The New Mortgage Game

ROBERT IRWIN

The New Mortgage Game

McGRAW-HILL BOOK COMPANY
New York St. Louis San Francisco Auckland Bogotá Hamburg
Johannesburg London Madrid Mexico Montreal New Delhi Panama
Paris São Paulo Singapore Sydney Tokyo Toronto

Irwin, Robert, date.
The new mortgage game.

Includes index.
1. Mortgage loans—United States. 2. Mortgage loans, Variable rate—United States. I. Title.
HG2040.5.U5I75 332.7'22'0973 81-18665
AACR2

1234567890 DODO 898765432

ISBN 0-07-032053-5

The editors for this book were William Newton and Christine Ulwick, the designer was Richard A. Roth, and the production supervisor was Teresa F. Leaden. It was set in Souvenir Light by IceType.

Printed and bound by R. R. Donnelley & Sons Company.

CONTENTS

About the Author

Robert Irwin, a California real estate broker for nearly 20 years, has guided many buyers and sellers through a variety of profitable real estate transactions. He has been a consultant to lenders, investors, and other brokers—helping to secure financing for transactions that might otherwise not have been made. He is also a highly successful private investor in the real estate market. Mr. Irwin is the author of six other McGraw-Hill books: *How to Buy and Sell Real Estate for Financial Security, Protect Yourself in Real Estate, How to Buy a Home at a Reasonable Price, Riches in Real Estate, The Real Estate Agent's and Investor's Tax Book*, and *The $125,000 Decision.*

PREFACE

Yes, you can get a good mortgage to buy the home you want! Yes, you can arrange financing to sell the house you must get rid of!

Chances are that both of these statements are true for you. Rumors to the effect that real estate financing is dead, to paraphrase Mark Twain, have been greatly exaggerated.

There are mortgages out there, and the key to buying the house you want—to selling your house—is to get one of them. But, the mortgages of today can be confusing. The good old days of going down to the local savings and loan association and getting a "standard" real estate mortgage are gone.

Today there are ARMs and SAMs and GPMs and PMIs and many more. It's enough to make a grown person cry. How can a determined buyer or a desperate seller make any sense out of this alphabet soup of mortgages? How does one know where to turn? What mortgage is the best mortgage for you?

Each month more than *$4 billion* is offered in real estate mortgages in the United States. The money is there, readily available for those who know how to get it. Are you getting your share?

Or are you one of those who hides his or her head in the sand and says, "I couldn't possibly qualify with interest rates this high." Or, "I can't tell the difference between an adjustable-rate mortgage and a shared-appreciation mortgage. It's just too confusing to handle."

Or even, "There's just nothing out there for me."

Nonsense!

Virtually anyone can get a mortgage of some kind today, often with lower-than-expected interest rates. Five percent down payments with low monthly payments are readily available *with only a single mortgage and no creative financing!* (Of course, if you want creative financing, it, too, is there. See Chapter 6.)

The key, of course, is knowing where to look and what to look for. That's why this book was written.

In this book we'll cover all the major new types of mortgages. We'll see how adjustable-rate mortgages (ARMs or VRMs) shared-appreciation mortgages (SAMs), graduated-payment mortgages (GPMs), and many more really work. We'll see who is best suited to get them and who should not take them. We'll see what their advantages are and what are the pitfalls to avoid. This book will help you make a money-wise mortgage decision.

In addition, we'll also cover creative or seller financing. We'll explore the world of "seconds" and "wraparounds" and "contracts for sale" and many more. We'll see how no-money-down and money-back-to-buyer on sale works. If you're a seller, this book will show you when you want to use creative financing and when you don't. If you're a buyer, you'll see how to make creative financing profitable for you.

Most of today's real estate mortgages did not even exist a year or two ago. They are totally new and different. They are part of a revolution that's taken place in real estate.

Today we are operating in a "new mortgage game." The old rules are out the window—new rules are in force.

If you don't know the new rules, if you try to play yesterday's game, you can get hurt in the wallet—badly. If you're contemplating spending the kind of money it takes to *buy* real estate today, if you're about to *sell* a home where the right kind of financing can mean thousands of dollars difference to you—you owe it to yourself to spend a few moments learning the "New Mortgage Game"!

Special Note to Reader

The opinions expressed in this book regarding the value of one type of financing over another are strictly those of the author. When making a financing or real estate decision, you should consult with your own real estate broker and an attorney who specializes in real estate law.

ROBERT IRWIN

The New Mortgage Game

ONE

How Much Should You Borrow?

There's a very old joke that goes something like this: Two entrepreneurs are contemplating buying a skyscraper in New York. One tells the other, "The building costs $60 million. The closing costs are $5 million. The rental income will be $500,000 a month."

"Sounds great," says the partner.

"There's only one problem," observes the first investor.

"What's that?"

"They want $500 in cash down."

In real estate the rule of the game has always been financing. Nobody but nobody ever seems to pay cash for property. There's always the down payment and then the mortgage. The smartest investors and home buyers have always been thought to be those who could get into their property with the least amount of cash.

Today, in the new mortgage game, getting the highest mortgage, going for the lowest down payment, doesn't always make sense. Today, putting more money down in cash and getting a smaller mortgage, ultimately, may result in a better investment, in more profit than the other way!

MORE WAS BETTER

How did we get the idea that a bigger loan on property was better?

The idea came about because, until the 1980s, more was indeed better, at least from a profit standpoint. Let's begin by considering how a typical home purchase went, from a financing viewpoint, just a few years ago.

Jack wanted to buy a home. After several weeks of looking he found a house that he liked. It cost $60,000. He determined to buy.

After years of saving, Jack had $20,000 saved in a savings and loan association. He planned on using that money to purchase his home. But, his real estate agent pointed out that it was possible to get financing for up to 90 percent of the purchase price. That meant that Jack only needed to put down $6000.

$60,000	$60,000	Price
× 90%		
$54,000	−54,000	Mortgage
	$ 6,000	Down payment

"But," Jack asked his broker, "won't I be better off putting more money into the house? I have $20,000 I can put down. Won't putting up more money reduce my monthly payments?"

Shirley, his broker, observed, "Of course it will reduce your monthly payments. But, it will be a bad investment move. You have to think of both your house and your money in terms of investments."

PYRAMIDING YOUR MONEY

"Look at it this way. You have $20,000. You can, indeed, stick it all into this house you want to buy. But, if you're really smart, since the minimum down payment is only $6000, you'll put only the minimum down. That will leave you with $14,000 (less closing costs) and you can use that money to buy one or two more houses!"

"But, I can only live in one house at a time," Jack observed.

"You're not thinking investment.

"Houses appreciate in value. Each year they are worth more money. Let's say that they go up 10 percent a year. If you buy one house at $60,000, your increase in investment, your profit, is $6000 at 10 percent a year. But, if you own three houses, your return is three times $6000 or $18,000. Now which would you rather have—a return of $6000 on your $20,000 investment or a return of $18,000 on the same money?"

Jack had to agree that Shirley had a good point. It was common sense to put as little down and buy as many houses as possible. Jack was doing what the old brokers used to call "pyramiding" his money.

WHAT MAKES REAL ESTATE PROFITS REALLY POSSIBLE?

But, why did it make sense to do this? Although the profit method is obvious, why does it actually work? The question I'm asking is similar to this: Although it's obvious that when we plug our toaster into an electrical outlet, the contraption will make toast, why does it happen? From where does the toaster get the power?

I'll leave you, the reader, to answer the question on toasters yourself. But, for real estate, the answer is that it works in part because of inflation, but mostly because of financing.

The deal that Shirley was offering Jack involved a mortgage for 90 percent of the value of the property for 30 years at a fixed rate of interest. Think what that means in an inflation economy.

To make things convenient, we'll assume an annual inflation rate of 10 percent and a mortgage rate of 10 percent. As we saw, with an inflation rate of 10 percent, the property will appreciate $6000 in one year (assuming it moves at the same rate as the general inflation).

$60,000	Property value	$60,000	
× 10%	Inflation		
$ 6,000	Increase	+ 6,000	
		$66,000	New property value

WITH A FIXED-RATE MORTGAGE, THE LENDER GETS NONE OF THE PROFIT

Because the buyer, Jack, has a fixed-rate, fixed-term mortgage, the lender does *not in any way* participate in that $6000 appreciation during the year. Jack gets it all.

The lender does, of course, get his own 10 percent interest. His loan amount on the property, as we saw earlier, is $54,000. But once the mortgage has been funded, that loan amount is fixed. It doesn't matter if the property has gone up in price from $60,000 to $66,000. The lender's interest in the property remains the same—$54,000.

For Jack this results in a whopping return on his investment. He's stuck $6000 down into the property and in the first year he gets a $6000 return. Anyway you look at it that has to be a 100 percent rate of return.

For the savings and loan that made the mortgage, that has to be the worst possible deal in the world. Why? Consider the effects of inflation on the lender's rate of return. The most the savings and loan could hope to get in a return on its money was $5400 (that's 10 percent of the $54,000 mortgage).

But, we also noted that inflation was moving along at 10 percent. That means that the $54,000 the lender gave in the mortgage lost 10 percent of its value, or $5400, during the year. The lender's return on investment was zero!

$ 5400	Maximum interest paid during year
−5400	Less loss in value of principal due to inflation
$ 0	Return on $54,000 investment to lender

It doesn't work out too well for the lender.

At this point, I'm sure many careful readers are asking, "Why would any lender make such a ridiculous loan?"

"DUMB" SAVERS MADE FIXED-RATE MORTGAGES POSSIBLE

For the answer to that we have to remember that most of the home mortgages came from savings and loan associations. They acted as intermediaries. "Investors" put money on deposit and the savings and loan loaned it out at about 2 percent over the interest they had to pay. The reason these lenders were willing to make such loans is that the depositors were willing to accept a low rate of return on their deposits. As long as the savings and loans could make 2 percent on the turnover (their operational margin and profit), it didn't matter to them what the interest rate on the mortgage was. They weren't making their money on the appreciation of the property. They were making it on the spread.

As long as depositors were willing to put their money into accounts earning 4½, 5¼, or even 7½ percent interest, the savings and loans could make 2 percent above their cost of money and make a profit. The depositors or savers were *subsidizing* the borrowers.

In truth, the reason the whole scheme worked for Jack when he bought his home was because an enormous group of savers was willing to deposit their money at ridiculously low interest rates. The money that Jack made, in fact, was in part, money that these savers lost.

As long as this system was in operation, it only made sense for Jack to put as little of his own money into a house or any other real estate investment and borrow as much as he could. Chances are the amount he borrowed would be at or even below the rate of inflation. And even if it weren't, because the interest rate and the term of the loan was *fixed*, as long as there was any inflation in the *value* of the property, he got credited with *all* of it. The lender got none of the property's "profit," so Jack would have been a fool not to buy as much property with high mortgages as possible.

And that, of course, is what happened during the last half of the 1970s. Jack and millions like him gobbled up as much property as they could. In fact, anyone who didn't buy as much property as was possible under such conditions is probably kicking himself or herself right now.

The decision on how much money to borrow, how high to leverage property, was an easy one in the old days. It was: leverage it as high as you could afford.

HOW HIGH CAN YOU AFFORD?

We'll get into the criteria for leveraging today, which are different from only a few years ago, in just a few moments. But first, let's consider from another viewpoint how big a mortgage to get. Let's consider it from the viewpoint of ability to pay back.

Ability to pay back was also based on the philosophy that "more is better" in terms of financing. That's how the popular notion of buying with "nothing down" came into existence. If more was better, then total, or 100 percent, financing was best. This was complete leverage. It allowed, or so many people were led to believe, for the maximum profits. (In some cases less than nothing down was promoted. In deals such as this the buyer not only got the property, but money back as well! We'll go into these in our chapter on creative financing.)

But, as leveraging is increased, as the buyer's initial interest in the property dips down toward nothing, another factor is introduced, and that is the mortgage payment. It is a fact of life, then and now, that the more you borrow, the more you must pay back. Where is the dividing line that occurs when it no longer becomes profitable to borrow more, simply because it is increasingly difficult to pay back the loan?

There are essentially two ways of looking at this. The first way is the buyer's income-to-mortgage payment ratio. This method of determining how much Jack, in our last example, could afford to make in a payment assumes that Jack is going to continue ownership of the property indefinitely in the future and that he will have to make the monthly mortgage payments out of his income.

Payback as Determined by Income

Jack is a steam fitter and he makes about $30,000 a year. His payments on a $54,000 mortgage at 10 percent for 30 years are $474 a month. Can Jack afford to make these payments from his income?

From out of the depression, the FHA came up with a ratio which eventually seemed to be etched in stone. It was a method of calculating if a buyer could indeed afford a particular payment. It was the famous "4 to 1"!

Without the melodramatics, the ratio simply said that a buyer could indeed afford to make a payment *if* that payment (including taxes and insurance) was no more than one-fourth of his or her monthly income.

On Jack's house, the monthly payment on the mortgage (principal and interest) comes to $474 a month. We'll assume another $150 for taxes and insurance, making a total payment of $625 a month. Jack earns $30,000 a year. Can he afford a $625-a-month payment?

The answer is simple to find. The $625 represents one-fourth of Jack's needed monthly income. So we just multiply $625 times four to find that needed income.

$ 625	
× 4	
$ 2500	Per month needed income

Does Jack qualify for this mortgage by this method?

His $30,000-a-year income breaks down to exactly $2500 a month. He does indeed qualify. He can afford the mortgage.

The 4-to-1 ratio was created many decades ago, and built into it was an allowance for food, clothing, transportation, medical costs, recreation, and other expenses. Economists and financial planners agreed that the ratio was necessary to ensure that a borrower could make monthly payments. (Today some lenders are accepting 3 to 1.)

GO-FOR-BROKE METHOD

There's another method of calculating how much of a mortgage a borrower can afford in terms of monthly payment, and I like to call it the "go-for-broke" (GFB) method. This is the method advocated by most of the people I've talked with who promote "nothing down" as the way to go.

The basic assumption that's made in this philosophy is that property is going to appreciate in value—appreciate significantly. In the go-for-broke philosophy, the buyer/borrower bets everything on that appreciation.

Here's how it works. The buyer of a piece of property no longer is concerned with the 4-to-1 or 3-to-1 ratios we were just discussing. Those ratios try to match a buyer's income over the long term with the monthly payments.

Under GFB philosophy, however, the buyer makes the asumption that he or she is not going to own the property indefinitely. In fact, the buyer is going to resell for the profit probably within 2 or 3 years at the longest.

If Jack, from our last example, were to use the GFB philosophy, here's how he could calculate it:

1. I'm going to sell for a profit in a maximum of 3 years.

2. Since the higher the value of the mortgage, the more money to be made (leverage), I'm going to look for as close to nothing down as possible.

3. I don't care what the monthly payments are, as long as I can make them for just three years!

Putting "Go for Broke" to Work

Instead of looking at a $60,000 piece of property, Jack now looks at one for $111,000 in, he hopes, a high-demand area, with a mortgage of roughly $100,000. The payments on this mortgage at 12 percent fixed-rate interest for 30 years are $1028 a month. (Remember, under the old ratio system even at 3 to 1, the maximum Jack can afford is $833 a month.) In addition, to increase his leverage so he in truth has to pay nothing down, Jack gets the seller of the property to carry back a second mortgage for $11,000 payable at $150 a month. His total payments when $200 more for taxes and insurance are added in come to:

First mortgage	$1028
Second mortgage	150
Taxes and insurance	200
Total Monthly	$1378

You'll recall that Jack was making $2500 a month *before* taxes. The payment on this house is *more than half* of his total income. After taxes, social security, pension, and union dues, he probably would have less than $700 a month to live on.

But, Jack still had the $20,000 in savings in the bank. If times get tough, he reasons to himself, he can always use some of that money to live on.

Why would Jack strap himself down to such horrendous payments? The reason is that he's "going for broke." He assumes that the house is going to appreciate at least 10 percent in value each year over the next 3 years. Since the house cost $111,000, that's a total increase of about $36,000. When he sells in 3 years (before costs of sale), he'll stand to make $36,000. All on no investment at all! (Remember, he bought the house for nothing down.)

IS A HIGH MONTHLY PAYMENT TOLERABLE FOR A PROFIT AT THE END?

Of course, Jack doesn't like to think how much of the money in the bank he'll spend to live on because of the high payments. Nor, does he like to think what would happen should he lose his job and not have any income. Nor does he ever question the biggest assumption of all, that the property might not appreciate as fast as he hopes. After all, Jack is "going for broke."

The GFB method of calculating how much of a monthly payment a buyer can afford was very popular in the late 1970s and early 1980s. It usually involved private financing, since most institutional lenders such as banks and savings and loans wouldn't lend to Jack on such a basis. But, there were plenty of private individuals, mostly sellers hungry to sell their real estate, that would go along.

Under the GFB method, *any* monthly payment is tolerable, as long as there's a profit to be made at the end of the road.

Does the go-for-broke method make economic sense today?

I obviously don't think so. Whatever sense it might have made a few years ago, it makes almost none today, particularly with the new kinds of financing available. The decision of "how much should I borrow" has to be made today with a whole new set of criteria.

THE NEW MORTGAGE GAME

The days of the "dumb" depositor are over. Savers will no longer put their money in savings and loan associations (S&Ls) and banks at low interest rates. They want the highest interest rates available. In order to stay in business, the S&Ls and banks have to pay competitive rates on their depositors' money.

To do this, they have to receive competitive rates on their mortgages. If they pay depositors 14 percent, they have to get something like 16 percent on their mortgages.

To make it all worse, savings institutions never know far in advance what the interest rate will be that they will have to pay! Today it could be 14 percent, tomorrow 16, by 3 weeks from now it could be down to 12. The interest they have to pay depositors fluctuates. Similarly, the interest they receive from mortgages will have to fluctuate to meet the depositors' demands.

The Great Liquidity Squeeze

As if the problems of the S&Ls and some banks weren't bad enough, with the advent of the money-market mutual funds offered by many stock brokers, people withdrew over $160 billion in deposits and put them into these new funds. Suddenly, the S&Ls had to sell their old mortgages to pay off their depositors.

How does an S&L "sell" a mortgage? Easy!

If I loan you $10 and you give me an IOU for that $10, I have something to evidence my loan—that piece of paper. Now, let's say I've agreed that you don't have to pay me back the $10 until next week. But, it's only Wednesday and I want to go to a movie and I need the $10 now. How do I get it?

Simple, I go down the street to a mutual friend of ours and I say, "I loaned out ten bucks. Here's the IOU. We both know the borrower's a good person and sure to repay. Won't you give me $10 now in cash in exchange for this 'marker,' this paper IOU?''

Our mutual friend thinks about it, then says, ''What's in it for me?''

I consider and then say, ''All right, just give me $9.50. You can collect the $10 next week and make 50 cents profit.''

A deal is struck. I have my cash and someone else has your note.

Anyone Can Sell a Mortgage

In real estate, it works the same way. When we borrow money to buy a house, we give the bank or savings and loan a mortgage, our IOU. Later (or sooner) if the bank needs money, it can sell that IOU to a mutual friend (a government-sponsored agency).

The government has three semipublic organizations to handle the purchase of mortgages in the secondary market. They are:

Federal National Mortgage Association (Fannie Mae)
Federal Home Loan Mortgage Corporation (Freddie Mae)
Government National Mortgage Association (Ginnie Mae)

Buying and selling in the secondary market worked well for nearly 40 years, until the inflation of the 1980s and the accompanying high interest rates put a kink into it. The early 1980s brought interest rates that roared up to meet inflation, dropped when people stopped borrowing, then shot up again when inflation came back.

I don't have to describe the roller coaster ride of the early 1980s. If you were awake in America, you experienced it. And so did the lenders. Suddenly S&Ls found they were paying 5 percent on many savings accounts while the money-market mutual funds (as we've seen) were paying closer to 20 percent.

Depositors in the S&Ls pulled out their money to put into the funds. Suddenly, the S&Ls and many banks were caught in an enormous liquidity squeeze. They had to have funds to pay their depositors. So, they tried to sell their assets, their vast numbers of mortgages, in the secondary market.

But, their old mortgages were for low interest rates—often 10 percent or less. The secondary market didn't want 10 percent mortgages when the primary market was 15 to 17 percent.

The S&Ls couldn't sell their mortgages unless they ''discounted'' them.

What's a discount? It's what I did when I sold your IOU for $9.50 to our mutual friend. I took a 50-cent discount. The S&Ls had to do likewise. But, instead of just 50 cents, their discount to get rid of those old mortgages was more like $3. It was a discount in terms of billions.

Think of the loss. During the early 1980s, dozens of S&Ls had to close their doors, either forced into unwanted mergers or simply declared insolvent by the depository insurance agencies.

The Lender's Lesson—Never Again

Going into the 1980s, if you were a lender, what would you have learned by this lesson? What is the one thing you would be sure you weren't going to do again?

The answer? You'd be sure you weren't going to get stuck with any more of those low-interest-rate mortgages. You were going to be sure your mortgages kept pace, in terms of interest rate, with the overall money market. You were going to be sure your mortgages had interest rates that were adjustable to keep up with short-term money rates.

THE NEW MORTGAGE GAME OF THE 1980s

That's exactly what happened. The savings and loans and the banks, to keep up with their depositors' demands, to keep from being illiquid, have done away, for all practical purposes, with the old fixed-rate mortgages. Today, as we will see in the following chapters, something called an adjustable-rate-mortgage, or ARM, has largely taken their place.

Today, the interest rates fluctuate on modern mortgages. The fluctuation occurs usually every 6 months to a year. That means that a borrower might take out a mortgage at 13 percent and 6 months later it might be 14 percent. After another 6 months it could be 16 percent and then, after another period down to 13 percent.

It's a real roller coaster.

But, for the lenders it's survival.

Adjustable mortgage rates mean that lenders (once adjustable rate deposits are in place) will be able to accommodate demands of depositors. They will be able to attract depositors to their doors. That will give them money to lend out and avoid a liquidity squeeze for them.

Additionally, if they do need money, they will be able to sell these adjustable mortgages in the secondary market without the huge discounts seen on the older fixed-rate mortgages.

Finally, and this is something which lenders don't often talk about, with many of the new mortgages, they will actually be able to join with the borrower/buyer of the property and share some of the profits. They will actually become the borrower/buyers partner in the new house!

The Lender as Partner

By increasing the interest rates, often fluctuating them according to other short-term rates, the lender actually *participates* in any profit the property may achieve.

This is a concept that few people truly understand, but it certainly is worth taking a moment to look at. Let's go back to Jack with his $54,000 mortgage on a $60,000 piece of property. You'll recall in our old example, that the interest rate on the mortgage was fixed at 10 percent and that inflation was also 10 percent. Jack profited very much from that mortgage.

But, let's assume that Jack buys the same piece of property today. Only today, the mortgage is an "adjustable" rate. It can move up and down depending on short-term interest rates.

Let's further say the Federal Reserve decides that a 10 percent inflation rate is too high. To curb inflation, it tightens up the money supply which forces short-term interest rates up to 20 percent. Suddenly, instead of paying 10 percent, Jack finds he's paying 17 percent on his new mortgage! How does that work out for his profit picture?

(We'll assume once again that the property appreciates 10 percent, or $6000, in value during the year.)

Maximum yearly payment on new 17 percent annual-rate mortgage	$9180
Maximum yearly interest payments on old 10 percent fixed-rate mortgage	– 5400
Additional payments on new mortgage	$3780
Profit from 10 percent inflation on house	$6000
Less additional mortgage payment	– 3780
Actual profit with new mortgage	$2220

The new adjustable-rate mortgage, which zoomed to 17 percent when the short-term interest rate rose, has eaten up $3780 of the $6000 appreciation that Jack had expected to receive on his property. Instead of a $6000 appreciation (profit), he now must be satisfied with only $2300. That's a considerable difference. It also makes the "broke" in the go-for-broke philosophy more likely to happen.

Transferring the Profit to the Lender

What we're observing here is not so much a loss of potential profit or appreciation, as a transference. The appreciation is still there. It's just that instead of Jack getting it *all* with the lender tied down by a fixed-term, fixed-interest-rate mortgage, now the lender is sharing. (Some of the new mortgages, in fact, are even called "shared-appreciation mortgages.")

This new factor makes a considerable difference when it's time to consider how much financing to place on a piece of property. In the old days, it was borrow as much as possible. But, today, when we borrow we get an unwanted partner, the lender.

Consequently, now it only makes sense *not* to borrow up to the hilt. Rather, the amount to be borrowed must be carefully balanced against at least three factors:

1. How much cash do we have to invest?

2. How much of a share of our profit are we willing to give the lender?

3. How much appreciation can we realistically expect from the property?

The decision for today involves moderation, not excess.

All of this, of course, is not to say that there's no profit to be made on real estate or that leveraging is bad. It's only to say that today, going for broke may mean just that!

TWO

Can You Get A Fixed-Rate Mortgage?

There are no more dinosaurs (at least not living ones) on this planet, and most lenders would have you believe that there are also no more fixed-interest-rate mortgages.

Nothing could be further from the truth. While they may not be readily available from the traditional lender, such as most savings and loans and banks, they are still available from many private lenders and a few savings and loans and banks. But, before we get specifically into where to find a fixed-rate mortgage today, let's spend a little time exploring the ins and outs of this type of loan.

DEFINITION OF A FIXED-RATE MORTGAGE

A fixed-rate mortgage is very simple to define. As applied to real estate, it's simply a mortgage in which the interest rate does not vary, but remains the same for the life of the mortgage. If the borrower on a fixed-rate mortgage gets an initial rate of 12 percent, that rate lasts for the life of the mortgage.

Having said that, there are a few more pointers that should be looked at that distinguish a fixed-rate real estate mortgage from other types of loans.

When a family buys a home and gets a new fixed-rate mortgage, they are generally getting a "first." We'll go into what that means in detail in a later chapter, but, for now, let's simply say that it means that it is the first mortgage to be put on the property. If that's the case, then usually the *term* of the fixed-rate mortgage will be for 30 years.

Term

*

"Term" refers to the duration or length of the mortgage. Thirty years is almost always used, and this term was chosen for a specific reason. To understand that reason, let's compare the monthly payments required to pay back a $100,000 fixed-rate mortgage at 12 percent interest for varying lengths of time.

$100,000 MORTGAGE AT VARYING TERMS AT 12 PERCENT INTEREST—MONTHLY PAYMENT

10 years	*15 years*	*20 years*	*25 years*	*30 years*	*35 years*
$1435	$1200	$1101	$1053	$1029	$1016

What should be obvious is that the *longer* the term of the loan, the *lower* the monthly payment. Most home buyers and other purchasers of real estate want the lowest monthly payment and, since extending the term *lowers* the payment, they go for the longest possible term. But, why was 30 years determined as the standard? Why not 50 or 500?

An obvious reason is that the collateral for the mortgage is the building, and most buildings wouldn't last 500 years and maybe not 100. (Studies have indicated that the actual lifespan of most buildings is close to 80 years!)

The not-so-obvious reason can be clearly seen when the monthly payments and term are plotted on a graph (Figure 2–1).

As we move from 10 to 15 to 20 years, we significantly reduce the monthly payment. However, as we approach a 30-year term, the amount of reduction in payment for each year added gets smaller. Once we reach 30 years, we are at the optimum point on the curve. Any further extensions of term reduce the monthly payment only insignificantly. For example, going from a 30-year term to a 35-year term, an addition of *5 more years* on the mortgage, only reduces the monthly payment by about *$13 a month.* Going from 30 years to a 40-year term would only reduce the monthly payment by about $20 per month! That's a savings of only $20 per month for an extension of the payback period for 10 full years!

It's easy to see why 30 years was chosen as the optimum period of payback time. (We'll see how this payback phenomenon affects

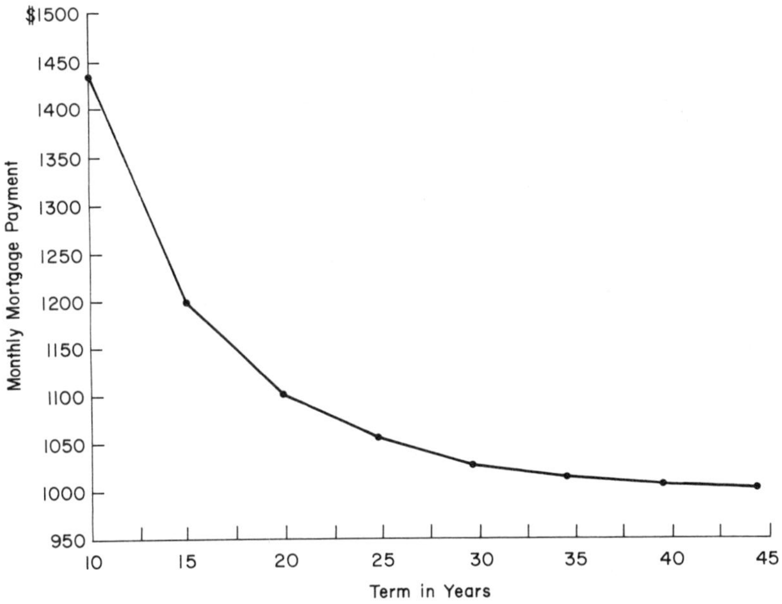

FIGURE 2–1. Fixed-rate mortgage: Term of mortgage versus monthly payment. Monthly payments decline dramatically as term is increased until year 30. From there, further increases in term do not significantly lower payment.

mortgages more significantly when we get to the variable-rate loans.) To get further significant reductions in the monthly payment, we'd have to go to increases of hundreds and then thousands of years!

Amortization

Most fixed-rate first mortgages with 30-year terms are fully "amortized." As those in the field know, that is a fancy term for a simple concept. It means that the payments are arranged so that the mortgage is fully repaid. In other words, there is no balloon payment or any individual payment larger than any of the others. (Occasionally, the final monthly payment may be a bit smaller than the others.)

A fully amortized mortgage looks like Figure 2–2.

Note that although the monthly payment remains the same for 359 payments ($1028.62), the amount that goes toward interest and the

Month	Balance	Interest	Principal
1	$99,971.30	$1000.00	$ 28.62
12	99,636.30	996.69	31.93
24	99,226.30	992.63	35.99
36	98,764.10	988.05	40.57
48	98,243.30	982.89	45.73
60	97,656.40	977.08	51.54
72	96,995.30	970.54	58.08
84	96,250.30	963.16	65.46
96	95,411.00	954.85	73.77
108	94,465.10	945.49	83.13
120	93,399.30	934.93	93.69
132	92,198.50	923.05	105.57
144	90,845.80	909.65	118.97
156	89,320.30	894.55	134.74
168	87,602.00	877.54	151.08
180	85,665.80	858.37	170.25
192	83,484.10	836.76	191.86
204	81,025.60	812.42	216.20
216	78,255.60	785.00	243.62
228	75,133.90	754.09	274.53
240	71,616.30	719.26	309.36
252	67,652.60	680.02	348.60
264	63,186.70	635.80	392.83
276	58,154.80	585.98	442.64
288	52,484.70	529.84	498.78
300	46,095.60	466.58	562.04
312	38,896.10	395.30	633.32
324	30,783.50	314.98	713.64
336	21,642.10	224.47	804.15
348	11,341.40	112.48	906.14

Final payment = $ 756.38
Total interest = $270,016
Total payments = $370,016

FIGURE 2–2. Principal versus interest of monthly payments for a fully amortized mortgage of $100,000 for 30 years at 12 percent. Monthly payment = $1028.62.

amount to principal change with each payment. On the first payment only $28.62 is a return of principal while $1000 is the interest charged. By payment 348 (year 29), however, about $900 goes to principal with only about $100 going to interest.

This means that the vast majority of the interest paid on the mortgage over its life is paid during the first years. Even after 10 years of paying, less than $100 per month is going to principal, more than $900 is still going to interest.

Increasing the amount paid to principal during the early years by voluntarily paying more each month can dramatically reduce the total interest paid over the life of the mortgage, as well as significantly cut the time required for full payback.

Note that after 30 years, when the full $100,000 has been repaid, the amount of the total interest charged during the time has been $270,016. The interest charged has been nearly three times the total amount borrowed! For higher interest rates than 12 percent, the total interest charged is also significantly higher.

How Amortization Works

Calculating interest on amount borrowed

$100,000		Mortgage amount
× 12		Interest rate
12,000		Annual interest
÷ 12%		Months/year
$ 1,000		First month's interest
	$1,028.63	Monthly payment
	−1,000.00	Interest
	$ 28.63	To principal

On a $100,000 mortgage at 12 percent a year fixed rate, the first month we pay $1000 in interest and we pay only $28.63 on principal, or on return of the money borrowed. It hardly seems possible we could ever pay it all back.

But, remember, this is just the *first month's* calculation. Each month that follows must be calculated differently:

Second month's payment calculation

$100,000.00	Original amount borrowed
− 28.63	Paid back first month
$ 99,971.37	Current amount owed

The amount owed at month two is less by exactly $28.63 from the amount owed at month one. Therefore, the calculation for interest is also different:

Interest calculated for month two

$99,971.37		Amount owed
× 12%		Annual interest rate
11,996.56		Annual interest
÷ 12		Months/year
$ 999.71		Second month's interest
	$1028.63	Monthly payment (remains the same)
	− 999.71	Interest
	$ 28.92	To principal

Two things are critical to see here. First, as we go into the third month, the amount of principal we have paid back will be the amount paid back in both months one and two:

$ 28.63	First month payback
+ 28.92	Second month payback
$ 57.55	Deducted from original $100,000 equals amount borrowed in third month

Second, the amount of the payment going to principal increases.

$ 28.93	Second month payback
−28.63	First month payback
$ .29	Increase in amount of principal payback in second month

Even though the increase after one month is only 29 cents, it is the compounding of this increase as the original amount borrowed is paid back over 30 years that repays the mortgage. Each month, the amount that goes to principal and interest changes. Each month, a little more goes to principal, a little less to interest. In later years, almost all the monthly payment goes to principal, virtually none goes to interest. (See Figure 2–2.)

Of course, we haven't come all this way just to see how a fixed-rate mortgage works mathematically. There is another reason, and that has to do with cutting monthly payments.

How to Cut Your Monthly Payments

Virtually all fixed-rate mortgages allow for the borrower to increase the amount of the monthly payment up to twice without penalty. (That is, without a prepayment fee, which we'll discuss shortly.)

Consider the effects on our 30-year mortgage of paying more than the amount due each month. Let's say that, initially, we double the amount of the mortgage payment that goes to principal.

Doubling principal payment

$ 28.63	First month's principal
× 2	Doubling
57.26	
1028.63	First month's payment
$1056.63	New amount paid

Instead of sending the lender the agreed-upon $1028.63, we send the lender more. In this case, the amount we send is double the amount due on principal, or $1057.63.

Needless to say this is going to cause the lender a headache. The payment schedule is carefully worked out at the time the mortgage papers are signed. By sending in additional principal, the borrower messes up all that paperwork. But, it can be changed by simply getting a new computer printout.

(*Caution:* When attempting this procedure, the borrower must indicate that the additional amount paid goes to reduce the principal. Otherwise, the lender could simply count it towards a prepayment of interest, which would do the borrower no good.)

Now, having paid an additional amount toward principal, let's see what effect this has on the second month's payment.

New calculation for second month

$100,000.00	Original amount borrowed
− 57.26	Paid back
99,942.74	New amount owed
× 12%	Interest rate
11,993.13	Annual interest
− 12	Months/year
$ 999.43	Monthly interest

Difference between interest charged

$ 999.72	Interest on old schedule
− 999.43	Interest on new schedule
$ .29	Interest savings

By paying an additional $28.63, we have saved the interest that would have been charged on that money, or the monthly amount of 28 cents.

Now, who would pay $28 to save 28 cents?

The answer is, it might be paid by someone who had some excess cash and who wanted to save a whole lot of money on interest in the long run. For the truth of the matter is that by doubling up the principal payment *each month,* the reduction in interest increases enormously so that, after a few years, the borrower isn't just saving a few cents per month, but hundreds of dollars. In fact, if the doubling were to be carried out for the life of the mortgage, the mortgage could be paid back in about half the time (15 years instead of 30) at a savings of thousands of dollars that otherwise would go toward interest. It's an incredible savings of more than half the total interest charged!

The key to this stratagem, of course, is being able to double the principal amount. In the early years of the mortgage, it's easy. We're only talking about an additional $28 per month here. But, in the later years of the mortgage, it would be paying virtually double the monthly payment, or almost $2000 a month.

(But, on the other hand, it could be argued that it won't get that high until 15 years later and, with inflation, it might not be so hard after all.)

What we are talking about, of course, is forced savings which could result, in about 15 years, in a completely paid-off property. Or, if sold in a lesser period of time, it could mean an additional amount of equity to the owner.

It's an interesting idea and, even if you decide not to do it, I think it goes a long way toward explaining how interest works with regard to a 30-year mortgage.

Prepayment Penalty

Lenders on mortgages were for many years concerned about a situation such as the one described above, although in a more extreme case. They were concerned with a borrower prematurely paying off a mortgage. This was primarily true during the days when lenders felt that the fixed-rate return from their mortgages was adequate.

It's easy to imagine this from a lender's viewpoint. The lender has gone to the trouble of checking out a borrower's credit and the proposed piece of property, and has issued the appropriate documents. Money has been transferred and is committed for a long number of years. Once all this has been done, the lender sits back and relaxes, knowing that the money is earning the determined interest rate.

Then, out of the blue, the borrower suddenly pays off the mortgage early (or a large part of it). The lender is faced with going through the entire process again with a new borrower and a new piece of property.

To discourage early or prepayment, many lenders began charging a "penalty" sometimes also called a "bonus" or "fee." Typically, on residential property this penalty was 6 months interest, and it only applied if the borrower paid back more than 20 percent of the outstanding mortgage balance in a single year.*

Six month's interest, if we go back to our $100,000 mortgage at 12

---

* Each mortgage is written differently, so yours might have a different set of conditions.

percent annually, could come to close to $6000. That's a hefty penalty and could discourage prepayment.

When the Lender Prohibits Prepayment

Some lenders *prohibit* the prepayment of a mortgage. This is often the case in commercial mortgages when the lender is an insurance company. Insurance companies often make mortgages when the amounts are in excess of half a million dollars and the property is a shopping center, office building, or other investment parcel. Once the insurance company commits to such an investment, it wants to be very sure that it is going to get its money back *exactly* as agreed upon. Frequently, its ability to maintain its solvency and service its insurance policies over the long term depends on this.

So the insurance companies tend to "lock in" their mortgages. In such a case, they will not allow any early payment of principal, *even with a penalty.*

(In recent years, however, with interest rates rising higher and higher, many insurance companies have been "induced" to negotiate their position by having the borrower offer one of three things: (1) a substantial bonus for early payment; (2) a new and higher interest rate on any remaining balance; or (3) part ownership in the property.)

"Due-On Sale" Clause

We mentioned the "due-on sale" clause (commonly called the "due-on" clause) briefly earlier, but it is worth a more thorough examination, particularly since more than two-thirds of the homeowners in this country still have fixed-rate mortgages containing such a clause. Here is a typical due-on clause*:

> In the event the "borrower" without the prior written consent of the "lender" sells, agrees to sell, transfers or in any way *alienates* its interest in the real property or any part thereof or any interest therein, the "lender" may at its option *accelerate* the mortgage and declare all sums secured hereby *due* and payable.

---

* In actual due-on clauses, the terms "borrower" and "lender" would be substituted by the words "mortgagor," "mortgagee" or "trustor" and "beneficiary."

The words that have been italicized are the critical ones here.

Alienate: This simply means to sell or in some way change the title to the property.

Accelerate: This means to speed up the payback of the mortgage. Instead of being due monthly, the principal amount would be due all at once. In other words, the mortgage would have to be paid off.

Due (on): This simply refers to the fact that the mortgage becomes payable upon sale of the property. The due-on clause was the safety valve that savings and loan associations had to help ensure their liquidity. Prior to 1979, they knew that statistically homes were resold on the average nationwide of every 7 years. (Roughly every 5 years in California, Florida, and a few other states.) With the due-on clause inserted, they felt assured that, when the property was sold, they could either call for all their money or jack up the interest rates to then-current levels. On the average, even though the mortgages were all written for 30 years, because of market habits, the longest they stood to have their money out at the old interest rate was 7 years.

However, in several court cases, but principally the *Wallenkemp* decision in California, state courts ruled that the due-on clause was unenforceable. Their reasoning seems to have been the following:

The ostensible purpose of the due-on clause was to protect the lender against the borrower selling the property to an uncreditworthy new buyer.*

However, the courts seemed to feel that as long as the new buyer or the borrower demonstrated a reasonable interest in the property, the S&L couldn't challenge the new buyer's creditworthiness. In other words, if the seller kept a sizable interest in the property as through a second mortgage or the buyer put up a substantial down payment, the due-on clause wasn't enforceable.

The safety valve for the S&Ls was clamped shut.

Fourteen states had similar rulings before the S&L industry began to lobby seriously for legislation to overthrow the restriction on the due-on clause. As of this writing the final outcome is still in doubt.

* The purpose of assuring liquidity was seldom mentioned.

Check with a broker or attorney in your own state for the status of the due-on clause in your area.

Interestingly enough, federally chartered banks and savings and loan associations were generally exempted from the restrictions on the due-on clause. Because the assumption was that federal law superseded state law, they were often allowed to enforce the clause, while state-chartered savings and loans and mutual banks located right next door could not. This will probably be decided finally by the U.S. Supreme Court.

WHY SHOULD YOU GET A FIXED-RATE MORTGAGE?

Advantages

The fixed-rate mortgages we've been discussing thus far are those aimed primarily at home buyers. However, what follows is also generally true for investors.

In most cases, the home buyer is *better off* going for a fixed-rate mortgage than any other kind. The reasons are fairly obvious and were spelled out in the first chapter.

1. The borrower knows in advance what the interest rate on the mortgage will be and what the monthly payments will be.
2. Any appreciation on the house due to inflation or other factors *all* goes to the buyer. None goes to the lender.
3. In a market in which interest rates are rising, a fixed-rate mortgage in which the due-on clause is unenforceable (that is, the mortgage can be assumed by a new buyer), is a big help in selling.

The first point is fairly obvious. In the other mortgages we'll be discussing, the interest rate and frequently the monthly payment can vary enormously. This puts a great strain on the person who is trying to maintain a budget.

The second point we've already discussed at length in the first chapter.

Fixed-Rate Mortgages Help You Resell

The third point, however, deserves a bit more attention. Although most buyers don't realize it, in a market in which financing is everything, *the time to prepare for selling a home is when you buy it.* What that comes down to is arranging for the financing that you will need to sell at the time you buy.

One method of doing this is to obtain a fixed-rate mortgage (one that is assumable). There are two advantages to doing this:

First, when it's time to resell, your buyer doesn't need to qualify for a new mortgage, which with today's high prices and high interest rates can be very tricky. (Normally, when there is already an assumable fixed-rate mortgage on the property, the new buyer only has to satisfy the seller. And the buyer putting up sufficient cash down usually satisfies most sellers.) Having an assumable loan means you're opening up your home to many, many more potential buyers.

Second, many buyers seek out *only* those houses with such mortgages on them. The new buyer is going to be just like you. He or she is going to realize the advantages of a fixed-rate mortgage. This means you have an additional bonus to offer a prospective buyer.

These financing bonuses can often be translated into dollars and cents. With an assumable fixed-rate mortgage, the seller can usually command a *higher price* than the seller who can offer only brand-new financing.

It must seem, therefore, that the fixed-rate mortgage only has plusses and that there are no minuses to it. If you can get one, should you always go for it? Not always.

Disadvantages of a Fixed-Rate Mortgage

There are a few minuses to the fixed-rate mortgage, although we haven't seen them in recent years.

The avantages of the fixed-rate mortgage came about principally because of the type of economic climate we've had in the recent past—high inflation and high interest rates. It only makes sense to opt for a fixed-rate 12 percent mortgage, if you believe that in 6 months time the interest rate will be 16 percent or higher.

But, what if inflation and interest rates drop? How does that affect the fixed-rate mortgage?

It can affect the fixed rate adversely. Consider the following scenario. Jill obtained a fixed-rate mortgage for 16 pecent interest. A year later with inflation down, interest rates fell to 10 pecent. New mortgages are then available at the 10 percent rate. How has Jill fared?

Not too well. She's stuck paying 16 percent, when new mortgages are going for 6 percent less. One big advantage to the fixed rate that we were just discussing (its plusses when it's time to resell) has just vanished. Instead of a plus, the fixed rate now is a headache—a definite minus.

What can Jill do?

About the only thing she can realistically do is to bail out. With rates as low as 10 percent, she's paying an enormous penalty by having a 16 percent mortgage. Consider the monthly payment differential.

$100,000 mortgage fixed rate at 10 and 16 percent

Monthly payment

10 percent = $877 16 percent = $1345

Jill is paying $468 more per month because she has a higher interest rate! Naturally, she'll want to pay off the old 16 percent mortgage and go for a new 10 percent one.

But, that could be difficult. For one thing, there's the early pay off penalty we were just discussing. On a $100,000 mortgage at 16 percent interest, the penalty could be whopping $8000. That might make her think twice.

Then, there's the matter of getting a new 10 percent loan. Jill must go through the entire procedure of qualifying again and so must her property. But, there's one big difference. Before she was a new buyer. Now she's an existing owner trying to refinance.

(In times of tight money, lenders tend to be very preferential about those to whom they loan money. Generally speaking, they'll make their mortgages first to new buyers and then, only if they have available funds, to refinances. Jill might have some trouble finding a lender to give her a refinance.)

The point here is that obtaining a fixed-rate mortgage at the *top* of an interest-rate cycle may actually be a disadvantage. At least when compared to other types of mortgages. One of the new mortgages we'll be discussing involves a variable rate. The interest rate goes *up or down* keyed to an index of short-term interest rates. Examples are usually given of such a mortgage going up 5 or 10 percent in a short time as interest rates rise. It can, with disastrous results as we'll see. But, if a borrower obtains such a mortgage at the *top* of the interest-rate cycle, the mortgage interest rate can plunge. If Jill had obtained a *variable* interest-rate mortgage at 16 pecent and the interest rate for short-term funds dropped to 10 percent, she'd soon be paying only 10 percent *without lifting a finger.* The mortgage rate would automatically come down.

The fixed-rate mortgage has many advantages, but it is not for everyone and not at all times. Even when you have the option of obtaining one, you should first examine both the other mortgages available as well as market conditions.

WHERE TO GET A FIXED-RATE MORTGAGE

As I noted when we began, the fixed-rate mortgage isn't dead as a dinosaur, but just about. To find one, you may have to do some searching. This could mean spending half a day or so calling a wide variety of sources. (It does not mean simply relying on a single banker or real estate agent. Both may have reasons for recommending a limited group of mortgage lenders, none of whom may have a fixed-rate mortgage.)

Your best bet is to cover the field. Simply go to the phone book and check the Yellow Pages under the following headings:

Mortgage *bankers* (not brokers)
Savings & loan associations
Commercial banks
Mutual savings banks
Credit unions
State housing or mortgage agencies*
City housing or mortgage agencies*

In a large city, you'll probably find hundreds of listings.

Ask to talk with a loan officer or loan broker. Start chatting. Oftentimes these professionals know not only what their own company offers, but what other companies have as well. If you're lucky, you may quickly hit one who can direct you right to a good source.

---

* To be discussed in the chapter on municipal mortgages.

THREE

Shared-Appreciation Mortgages —The Low Monthly Payment Mortgages

Shared-appreciation mortgages (SAMs) are probably the most exciting of the new mortgages to come over the horizon. When first introduced in Florida and New York, they made the headlines in *The Wall Street Journal* and other leading newspapers. They were touted as revolutionary and as a panacea to the mortgage crisis. Neither evaluation was entirely correct, but SAMs have offered something that no other mortgage has—***big** reductions in monthly payments.*

A BIG CUT IN MONTHLY PAYMENTS

To see just what the effect of a SAM really is, let's make a comparison between it and a conventional fixed-rate mortgage.

Fixed-rate mortgage—$100,000 at 14 percent for 30 years

Monthly payment	$1185	(30-year amortization @ 8½ percent interest)
Monthly payment	− 769	(SAM)
Reduction	$ 416	

If you have trouble believing your eyes, please understand you are reading the figures correctly. With the old fixed-rate mortgage, the payments are just about $1200 a month. With the SAM they are under $800. Is there any wonder that the SAMs drew crowds to whatever lenders offered them?

But, there's more to real estate financing than monthly payments, and there's more to a SAM than meets the eye at first glance. A borrower has to first ask, how can a lender afford to reduce the payment by so much? Where is the lender making up the difference?

The answer has to do with how the SAM operates. While it does cut monthly payments and interest, it makes it up by taking a share of the profit when the property is sold. Since most buyers have investment as an important consideration, this is a point well worth seriously considering.

SHARING APPRECIATION WITH THE LENDER

Insurance companies have long had a kind of equity-participation mortgage that they use with developers of shopping centers and other commercial investment ventures. These mortgages involve the lender receiving back not only interest, but a share of the ownership in exchange for making the mortgage. It is this concept on which the SAMs are patterned.

In a SAM, the lender offers the buyer/borrower a big initial reduction in the interest rate. However, in exchange for this favor, the lender then requires that this buyer/borrower share in the appreciation of the home. In other words, "I give you a break when you buy; you give me a break when you sell." (The "I" here is obviously the lender.)

It's not so much that, in a SAM, the lender is charging any less interest. It's that the lender, instead of getting all the money back in the form of interest, gets some in interest and some in the form of profit on the property. When you get a SAM, you get a partner.

The Differences Between a SAM and a Fixed-Rate Mortgage

There are at least three aspects of a SAM that differ significantly from a fixed-rate mortgage and should be considered carefully.

Interest rate versus profit shared

The interest rate on a SAM is less than that on a conventional mortgage. This is to say that it is less than the market rate at the time. If the market, for example, is at 14 percent for home mortgages, a SAM might be anywhere from 10 to 40 percent less. In the example of the $100,000 mortgage we took earlier, the interest rate on the SAM was 40 percent less, or 8½ percent.

Typically, in SAMs, the percentage the interest rate is reduced is also the percentage of the equity appreciation that the lender shares. If the mortgage interest rate is dropped by 40 percent, then the lender gets 40 percent of the equity when the property is sold.

It should be noted that this 40/40 split is the most popular at this writing, but it is most certainly not fixed in stone. One-third/one-third splits are also common as are some 10/10s. It is usually a matter of decision between both the lender and the borrower (although some lenders have fixed policies from which they will not budge).

Amortization—a hidden trap

In most cases, SAMs are amortized on the basis of 30 years. As we saw in our example of a $100,000 mortgage in the last chapter, that means that the monthly payment is calculated in such a way that the mortgage will be fully repaid in 30 years.

However, in almost all cases of SAMs, the mortgage is due back to lender *not in 30 years but in 10!* (Or less!)

This is a critical fact that some borrowers hear, but don't understand. Just because the payment schedule is based on 30 years doesn't mean that the mortgage is due in 30 years. With the old fixed-rate mortgages, 30 years meant 30 years. But, with today's new mortgages, having a 30-year amortization term just means how big your *initial* monthly payments will be. It doesn't mean that those payments will fully pay off the mortgage.

What happens after the end of 10 years?

At the end of 10 years, the entire mortgage is due and payable. However, typically it is not just the unpaid balance that is due. It is the unpaid balance *plus* additional interest.

When "contingent" interest comes calling: To understand the payoff after 10 years, we must first broach the subject of "contingent" interest. It's very simple to grasp. A SAM has two kinds of interest. The first kind is the interest actually charged. In our example, that was the 8½ percent on the mortgage.

The second interest is the contingent interest, or that which the lender hopes to get from (i.e., contingent upon) the equity appreciation in the property. That interest will be based on whatever the house appreciates to in value when the buyer eventually sells. (In the event the buyer doesn't sell, at the end of 10 years, that contingent interest is usually figured as the difference between the price at the time the house was bought and the appraised value at 10 years.)

$100,000	Market price at time of purchase
– 250,000	Appraised value at year ten
$150,000	Appreciation

At the end of 10 years, the lender would calculate 40 percent of the appreciation as based on an appraisal, and call that contingent interest. Forty percent of $150,000, or $60,000, would be due the lender.

One thing should be perfectly obvious. At the end of the 10-year (or less) period, the borrower is going to have a whopping big amount of money due to the lender. He or she will owe not only the unpaid balance of the mortgage, but all the contingent interest.

Refinancing out of a SAM

The final way a SAM differs significantly from a conventional fixed-rate mortgage has to do with refinancing. Nearly all lenders provide a guaranteed refinancing plan at the end of 10 years. This simply means that when the 10 years are up, the borrower isn't in the position of having to dig deep in his or her pocket to come up with cash. Instead, the lender has to allow the borrower to work out a new mortgage.

The lender, however, at this 10-year point, does not have to give the borrower preferential mortgage conditions. Typically, the refinance is at current market interest rates and the term is for the unpaid portion of the original mortgage (20 years).

If, after 10 years, the unpaid balance on our mortgage happens to be $93,399 (see Figure 2–2) and the contingent interest is another $40,000, the new mortgage would be for both these, or a sum of $133,399. The lender would then finance this amount at then-current interest rates for 20 years. (Some lenders, however, have indicated that at that time they would insist on a variable-rate mortgage, which will be discussed in the next chapter.)

WHO BENEFITS MOST FROM SAMs?

Let's take a look at the potential borrowers of SAMs.

Obviously, this mortgage is not for everyone. While at first it sounds like a panacea, some of its conditions, notably the equity sharing and the refinance after 10 years (or less) are not features with which everyone wants to get involved.

But, there is one feature of a SAM that is most attractive—the reduced initial monthly payment. As we saw, the monthly payment can come down by as much as 40 percent. This reduction should be of benefit mainly to two groups of people.

SAMs for First-Time Borrowers

Young couples or individuals who are buying their first home are in a particularly difficult spot in today's market. High prices mean that they have to come up with sizeable amounts of money to make the down payment. And high interest rates mean they have to have an enormous income to handle the high mortgage payments.

This is in contrast to second-time home buyers. These are people who already own their own home and are selling it to purchase another. In the process of selling, they usually obtain a substantial amount of cash (or paper) that they can use as a large down payment on a new home. The large down payment, by reducing the amount borrowed, also reduces the monthly payment, usually to a point where it can be managed.

But, for the young couple or individual starting out with the first house, the high down payment and huge monthly payments may be insurmountable obstacles.

The SAM offers little help in terms of reducing the down payment (the borrower will still probably have to come up with at least 10 percent down). But, it goes a very long way toward reducing the monthly payment and making it affordable. Consider the difference in qualifying between a conventional fixed-rate mortgage and a SAM:

Fixed-rate mortgage—$50,000 at 14 percent for 30 years

Monthly payment =	$ 592	Principal and interest
	+ 150	Taxes and insurance
	742	
	× 4	(4 to 1 qualifying ratio)
	2,968	Monthly income required
	× 12	Annualized
	$35,616	Annual income required

To obtain this loan, the annual income required would be over $35,000 a year. Now, let's consider the same $50,000 in a SAM:

SAM—$50,000 at 8½ percent amortized for 30 years (due in 10)

Monthly payment =	$ 384	Principal and interest
	+ 150	Taxes and insurance
	534	
	× 4	(4 to 1 qualifying ratio)
	2,136	Monthly income required
	× 12	Annualized
	$25,632	Annual income required

The difference is enormous, almost exactly $10,000 less needed in annual income for the SAM than for the conventional mortgage.

What this means is that SAM offers a way into real estate for those whose incomes are relatively modest, but who expect their incomes to rise within 10 years (remember the due date). A young couple or individual just starting out fills the bill perfectly.

Elderly Buyers

I've heard it argued that SAMs are also attractive to elderly buyers because it allows them lower payments at a time when they have a reduced income (because they are on pensions). I am not convinced of the wisdom here because of the 10-year due date. People on fixed incomes are in a bad position to take out a SAM if they intend holding the property. What is such a person to do at the end of the 10-year period?

In our example above, we assumed that monthly payments would be $534 for the initial 10 years. But, after that time, a refinance is in order. What if the property appreciated at an annual rate of 10 percent per year? At that time, it would be worth roughly $162,000 ($100,000 in appreciation). Of that amount, assuming the lender got a 40 percent share, the contingent interest would be worth about $40,000. If we assume that the original mortgage was paid down to $45,000 during this time, the borrower would now have to refinance a mortgage of $85,000. If interest rates then were comparable to now, that might be a rate of between 12 and 18 percent. We'll pick 14 percent as a likely rate:

$85,000 mortgage at 14 percent for 20 years = $1057 monthly

The elderly individual or family who had been paying $534 monthly would find that their monthly payments had doubled to $1057 monthly.

Would their pension payments and other income during retirement have also doubled during the same period? Judging from retirees during the last 10 years, that is doubtful. The retired person might be forced to sell the property because the payments would be an intolerable burden. And that's why I feel SAMs may not be for all elderly buyers.

A SAM AS AN INVESTMENT

There's a whole group of people for whom SAM may turn out to be a particularly unpopular mortgage. That is the repeat homebuyer, the individual or family who has sold a house and is in the process of buying another. For them, a SAM may prove to be particularly unappealing.

The reason is investment.

Nearly everyone buys real estate with an eye toward making some money on it. In fact, I have not met a single person in the last 5 years who didn't think of investment *first* when it came to property. From an investment perspective, a SAM could turn out to be a highly indesirable mortgage.

The thing about a SAM that is so different from a conventional mortgage when looking to investment, is that the contingent interest in a SAM is *unlimited*! In a conventional mortgage, the borrower knows exactly how much interest is going to be paid over the course of the mortgage on the day the mortgage papers are signed.

But, with a SAM, the contingent interest won't be known until either the property has been sold or the 10-year period is up. And this should worry a buyer.

Let's say that a buyer is very shrewd or very lucky and purchases a house with a $100,000 mortgage in an area where prices appreciate very rapidly. At the end of 3 years the house is worth $300,000. (Such rapid appreciation has occurred in scores of high-demand areas across the country.) We'll say the original purchase price was $120,000.

$300,000	Sales price
−120,000	Purchase price
$180,000	Appreciation

Our buyer purchased the home with a SAM. The SAM calls for a 40 percent participation. Upon sale at the end of 3 years, our buyer must now give the lender 40 percent of $180,000.

$180,000	Appreciation
× 40	Share ratio
$72,000	Lender's share

The lender's share of the appreciation comes to $72,000.

But, to see how much this really is we must now compare this amount with the amount the lender took off the mortgage in interest-rate reduction.

The mortgage was 8½ percent of $100,000. Therefore, the savings to the borrower was 5½ percent. (A 14 percent market rate was assumed.) Over the course of 3 years, that comes to approximately $16,000. The lender has reduced the buyer's payments by approximately $16,000 in interest. But the buyer/owner upon sale must share $72,000 with the lender!

$72,000	Lender's portion upon sale
−16,000	Lender's reduction of interest
$56,000	Lender's profit and buyer's loss on SAM

By taking the SAM instead of a mortgage at the market interest rate, the borrower/buyer has lost $56,000 in potential profit. It's easy to see why some buyers shy away from a SAM.

Of course, our example is exaggerated. Our house appreciated at an enormous rate. In the real world, most property can't be expected to appreciate quite so fast. In order to determine whether or not a SAM makes sense for you, you must first guess what the rate of appreciation will be for the property you are purchasing. If it's high, a SAM may not be desirable. In some cases, however, particularly depending on area, appreciation may be low, and then a SAM may make sense.

Let's consider a case in which our house only appreciated two percent a year, as has been the case in some neighborhoods.

At the end of 3 years, our original $120,000 house is now worth only about $127,000. The appreciation is just $7000, of which we must share 40 percent, or only $2800, with the lender.

$16,000	Lender's reduction of interest
−2,800	Lender's portion of sale
$13,200	Lender's loss of interest

Here the SAM made great sense for the borrower.

In addition to the considerations just made, anyone contemplating getting a SAM must also take into account at least four other items: additions to the property, destruction of the property, costs of sale, and redlining.

IMPROVING THE PROPERTY

Traditionally, once a person buys a home, even one with a mortgage on it, that home is his or hers to do with as desired, as long as the mortgage payments are made. If the homeowner wants to add a swimming pool or a second bathroom, he or she can do it without consulting with the mortgage company. (Most mortgages, however, provide that if the home is torn down or *reduced* in any way, the lender must first give permission.)

With a SAM, however, the waters get muddied. If a homeowner, for example, adds a new bedroom at a cost of $10,000 to a home, shouldn't that decrease equity by an equal amount on sale? For example, Henry bought a house for $100,000, added a bedroom at a cost of $10,000, and later sold for $150,000. What is his equity appreciation from the sale of the house? Is it $50,000 or $40,000?

Henry would certainly argue that it was $40,000. After all, he paid $10,000 out of his pocket for the cost of the room. However, Henry had a SAM and the lender didn't know about the room addition. Since the original purchase price was $100,000 and the sale was $150,000, the lender assumed that the equity appreciation was $50,000 of which it was entitled to its share.

To avoid problems such as these, most lenders have a clause in their SAMs which relate specifically to improvements. Usually the clause states that the cost of capital improvements may be subtracted from the appreciation. In Henry's case such a clause would mean that the appreciation would be only $40,000, not $50,000.

However, these same lenders are concerned that a homeowner may spend a great deal of money making improvements to the property (adding items to it) which are not justified. For example, adding a swimming pool to a home in Minneapolis or a fourth bathroom to a house in California could be a financial mistake (although the owner might justify the additions for personal reasons). The additions in this case probably would add less to the value of the home than they cost. The result would be that, on sale, the additions would actually *reduce* the amount of contingent interest to the lender.

In Henry's example, we assumed that the entire cost of adding the extra bedroom was reflected dollar for dollar in the sales price. But, now let's assume Henry had instead added a new entrance hall at a cost of $10,000 and this entrance hall only returned half its cost on sale.

	Adding extra bedroom	Adding new entrance hall
Cost	$ 10,000	$ 10,000
Added value on sale	10,000	5,000
House without addition	+ 140,000	140,000
Sales price	$150,000	$145,000

In the case of the bedroom, the addition added $10,000 to the price. But, in the case of the entrance hall, the addition was only

$5000. This reflected adversely on the lender's interest in the property.

	New bedroom	New entrance hall
Sale price	$150,000	$145,000
Original house cost	− 100,000	− 100,000
Appreciation	50,000	45,000
Less cost of improvement	− 10,000	− 10,000
Net appreciation	$ 40,000	$ 35,000

Because Henry's second improvement was not justified in terms of added value to the property, the lender had less equity to split up.

To counter this problem, many lenders of SAMs provide that *no* improvement may be made without the prior specific consent of that lender. If Henry wanted to add a room or an entrance hall, he would have to consult the lender. The lender would then make an appraisal (probably at a nominal cost to Henry) and determine whether it would be allowed. Undoubtedly, the lender would have a list of certain items that are justified in its area and others that are not.

In any event, Henry would find that his "right" to do with his property as he wished had been reduced. His "partner" now would require a say in any additions. It's something to keep in mind if you're considering a SAM.

DESTRUCTION OF THE PROPERTY

Many homes each year are destroyed by fire, wind, flood, earthquake, and other causes. To protect their interests against such an occurrence, lenders require that homeowners carry appropriate insurance, normally just enough to cover the mortgage amount. If the house is destroyed, the insurance company pays off and the lender gets its money back.

But, in the case of a SAM, there could be difficulties. While an insurance company would certainly pay off the outstanding mortgage amount, what about the contingent interest? How would the lender get that back?

In most SAMs, a provision states that the lender gets its percentage of whatever is left after the insurance company pays off.

In most cases, what is left is the land. Normally, the insurance company pays off the mortgage and the owner ends up with a burned-out lot. About the only time the owner gets more is if the home was insured for more than the mortgage value.

But with a SAM, the owner is still not done with the lender even after the insurance company has paid off the mortgage principal! If the lender is entitled, for example, to one-third of the equity appreciation, the owner may be forced to sell the lot or even give the lender a portion of excess insurance payoff to satisfy the agreement.

For example, let's say Henry bought a home for $100,000 with an $80,000 first mortgage, a SAM. At the time his house burned down, it was estimated to have been worth $120,000. How much money does Henry owe the lender?

Henry's liability to lender

$80,000		Mortgage outstanding
	$20,000	Appreciation
	× 40%	Lender's ratio
+ 8,000	$8,000	Contingent interest
$88,000		Amount Henry owes on destruction of home

When his house burns down, Henry owes the lender $88,000. But, since the outstanding balance on the mortgage was only $80,000, that's the amount the insurance covered. It also means that Henry has to dig into his own pocket to come up with the additional $8000!

This is not quite as bad as it seems. Usually, it is possible to obtain additional insurance to cover contingent interest. Again, it's something to seriously consider.

COSTS OF SALE AND CALCULATING EQUITY APPRECIATION

This is a fine point, but a tricky one. How is the equity appreciation actually calculated in a SAM?

Helene buys a home for $100,000 with an $80,000 SAM on it and later sells for $150,000. What is the equity appreciation which Helene must share with the lender?

For simplicity, thus far in this chapter, we've been assuming it's the difference, or $50,000. But, is it really?

The cost of purchasing the house (title insurance, escrow and recording fees, transfer taxes, etc.) may have been $2000. The costs of selling the house, including a real estate broker's fee, may have been $10,000.

Sales price	$150,000		
Purchase price	−100,000		
Gross appreciation	$50,000		
		$ 2,000	Purchase costs
		10,000	Sales costs
	− 12,000	$12,000	Total costs
Net appreciation	$38,000		

The costs of purchase and sale are real costs that Helene actually paid. The money she received was in the form of *net* appreciation. That's the amount on which she should base her sharing with the lender.

The point here is to be sure that when you sign up for a SAM, the agreement states that the shared amount is going to be based on *net* appreciation and not *gross*. One word can make a lot of difference moneywise.

REDLINING

"Redlining" is the term for refusing to issue mortgages in certain depressed areas allegedly practiced by some lenders in the early and mid-1970s. It was charged that, because some areas of every city were high-demand and others were low-demand, to protect their interests, some lenders only issued mortgages in the high-demand areas. Since the low-demand areas tended to be ghettoes, slums, and blighted districts, it was felt that such action would prevent them from ever changing their characteristics. Legislation outlawing redlining virtually eliminated any that existed by 1980.

SAMs however, may bring a form of redlining to real estate, even where it has never existed before.

In the past, lenders were primarily concerned with getting their money paid back. In a sense, they didn't care where they loaned, as long as the money was repaid. With a SAM, however, this is no longer the case. With a SAM, the lender has a vested interest in the appreciation of the property.

Let's take a city with two distinct districts. In Alpha district, prices are appreciating at 15 percent a year. In Beta district, they are appreciating at only 5 percent a year. If you were a lender offering a SAM on which you would benefit to the extent of 40 percent of appreciation, which district would you choose—Alpha where you would get 40 percent of 15 percent annually, or Beta where you would get 40 percent of 5 percent annually? If you chose Beta, it would explain why you're not a lender.

The tendency to offer SAMs only in high-demand areas by lenders is one additional problem that will have to be handled through the mid-1980s.

WHERE DO I GET A SAM?

Finding a SAM in some areas may be even harder than finding a fixed-rate mortgage. They are offered, but only by some lenders and then only sporadically. It's not hard to understand why.

A SAM offers a lender a low cash flow during its initial stages. The lender may be receiving back only two-thirds to 60 percent of the market mortgage rate during the initial 10 years.

For a savings and loan that must pay depositors out of mortgages, this can be an untenable situation. Savings and loans need a high cash flow during the entire duration of the mortgage. Therefore, S&Ls are unlikely offerers of SAMs.

On the other hand, SAMs are a tempting mortgage for the lender who doesn't have such cash-flow problems. Having some SAMs in an overall portfolio of mortgages gives a lender some protection against sudden shots of inflation. During inflationary periods, home prices tend to accelerate upward and equities increase. The lender who has SAMs can participate in this appreciation. SAMs therefore, can be highly desirable. But, what kind of lender can afford the long-term nature of a SAM (initial lean cash flow followed by a big cash flow after 10 years)?

The answer is some insurance companies and pension funds.

Insurance companies and pension funds have their income plotted over a long term and have the ability to make investments over the long haul. They are not so much concerned about the year-to-year return, as are savings and loans, but are concerned about the total yield after 10 or 20 or even 30 years. For them, a SAM makes a lot of sense.

Some large banks, which handle huge sums of money, both their own and investors, are in a similar position.

Therefore, if you want to find a SAM, there are essentially three major sources to look to—insurance companies, pension funds, and some banks.

Determining whether banks offer SAMs is easy enough. Just start calling the loan officers at your local banks. They'll tell you soon enough.

Finding out about insurance companies and pension funds, however, can be more difficult. These lenders almost never deal directly with the borrower when the amount is less than $500,000. To find out about these two lenders, it's necessary to first check with the people who place mortgages for them. These people are the *mortgage bankers*. They are listed under that title in the Yellow Pages of the phone book.

Finally, there is one last source to check, although it is most unlikely. Some savings and loans act as funnels for insurance companies and pension funds. The S&L initially funds the mortgage, but within a month sells it to the actual lender. Usually, such S&Ls, if they offer SAMs, will heavily advertise the fact.

SAMs are not for everyone. But for the person who can't buy a home any other way, they are a godsend.

FOUR

Adjustable-Rate Mortgages —the Only Game in Town?

How do you come up with a mortgage that will satisfy all the needs of both borrower and lender?

Obviously, you can't. So the lenders got together with their regulatory agencies and decided that, since they couldn't satisfy everybody, they would at least satisfy themselves. They came up with a mortgage that, they hope, will satisfy all the needs of the lender. And, since it may soon be the only mortgage that lenders offer, they hope that borrowers will go along.

The borrowers, home buyers, investors, builders, and so on, faced with accepting either this new loan or no loan, have begun to accept it. They've found that, while it usually isn't as good, from the borrower's viewpoint, as a fixed-rate, low-interest mortgage, it isn't all that terrible either. The name of this new mortgage is the ARM (adjustable-rate mortgage).

WHAT'S IN A NAME?

We'll get into the ARMs in just a moment, but first, let's consider their name. This is important because ARMs go by several different names. In the past, a form of this mortgage which was popular in many states was the variable-rate mortgage (VRM) or, as it was sometimes also called, the variable interest-rate mortgage (VIR).

Additionally, the Federal Home Loan Bank Board, which governs federal savings and loan associations, uses the term adjustable mortgage loan (AML) for this same mortgage.

When we use the term ARM here, we are, for practical purposes, also speaking of VRMs, VIRs, and AMLs. Although the first two were considerably different in operation from the current ARM, they are generally no longer offered, and their name has transferred to this new mortgage.

There is one other name we need to consider, and that is the renegotiable-rate mortgage (RRM). This mortgage was a predecessor of the ARM. When the ARMs came into existence, the RRMs went out. (Although a version called the "bullet" is back in as we'll discover shortly.)

HOW THE ARM WORKS

Peter and Helga live in North Carolina and they've just decided to buy a new home. But, before they go to look, they want to know just what kind of financing they can get. After all, this will determine how much they can afford for their new property.

Peter and Helga go to their local savings and loan association, where the loan officer informs them that she can give them a choice of two mortgages. One is the old-fashioned fixed-rate, 30-year mortgage, the other is the ARM.

"What's the difference?" Peter asks.

The loan officer is Sarah and she says, "The big difference for the home buyer/borrower is that on the old-style mortgage we are offering a 15 percent interest rate. But on the new ARM we are offering a 13 percent rate. (We'll see the reason for the differential later.) Here's what your initial monthly payments would look like if you borrowed on a fixed-rate mortgage and on an ARM.

MONTHLY PAYMENT COMPARISON BETWEEN FIXED-RATE AND ARM (\$100,000 Mortgage Amount)

	Fixed rate @ 15%	*ARM @ 13%*
Monthly payment	\$1260	\$1106

"As you can see, there's a \$154 monthly difference between the two mortgages. Initially, it would cost you far less to get the ARM."

"That's great," said Helga. "We certainly can use payments as low as possible. Are there any other differences?"

"Yes," Sarah pushed on. "The major difference between the two types of mortgages is that on the ARM, the interest rate is adjustable."

Adjustable Interest Rates

"Maybe you better explain that in more detail,"Peter asked. "How can an interest rate be adjustable?"

"When I say adjustable,"Sarah continued, "I really mean that the rate of interest on the mortgage can move up and down. Unlike the *fixed-rate* mortgage, the *adjustable-rate* moves up and down depending on market conditions."

"You mean," Peter leaned forward attentively, "that although we start with an interest rate of 13 percent, we could end up with an interest rate of 15 percent?"

"Yes, that's possible. Although it could go the other way, too. If market conditions are such that interest rates fall, the rate you pay could drop."

"But,"Helga asked with a worried look on her face, "how would we know when you might decide to raise or lower the rates? If you suddenly decide to jump up the rate 2 or 3 percent, it could be quite a shock."

Sarah smiled comfortingly. "We don't arbitrarily decide to raise or lower the interest rate. In our savings and loan, your interest rate is locked into the 90-day interest rate on U.S. Treasury bills. When the rate for the bills goes up, so does your mortgage interest rate. When T-bills go down, your mortgage rate follows."

"These floating rates could make me seasick," Helga said.

"If you think about it," Sarah concluded, "it is only fair. We have to pay our depositors based on short-term interest rates. Therefore, since the money we get to pay our depositors comes from interest on mortgages such as the one we may give you, we have to charge you interest based on the short-term rates. If we couldn't get the money from your mortgage to pay our depositors, we couldn't afford to stay in business."

Worrying About the Monthly Payment

"The only thing that's important to me," Peter leaned forward to emphasize his point, "is what the monthly mortgage payment will be. You say that our payments will be $1106 per month. As long as it stays at that amount, I don't care what you do with the interest rate."

Sarah sighed. "Unfortunately, that's not possible. You see, as the interest rate goes up, you will owe more money on the mortgage. It has to be paid. Similarly, as the rate goes down, you'll owe less. Your monthly mortgage payment will rise and fall depending on short-term interest rates..

"You mean our payment will change every month?" Peter shouted.

"No," Sarah laughed. "We make changes only every 6 months. And it's not so terrible. We've prepared a chart to show how it might work out over 5 years, if interest rates were to move up and down in the big cycles as they did between 1978 and 1981.

Year	*Interest rate*	*Monthly payments*
1	13	1106
2	15	1260
3	14	1186
4	16	1340
5	13½	1145

"As you can see, the most you would have to pay, based on past cycles, would have been $1340 which is only $234 more than your lowest payment. For most of the time, your payments would have been within $100 of your original payments."

"Of course, no one can predict the future. The rates could go up much higher. Or, as some economists I've heard are predicting, they could level off or even drop."

"As I see it, then," Peter concluded, "with the adjustable-rate mortgage, it's a gamble. We're gambling our monthly payments that the interest rates will either stay level or drop. We lose if they go up."

"That's one way of putting it."

Not all borrowers would like to take the gamble on an ARM. But, I think this dialogue does offer several insights into what an ARM is and some of its immediate problems as well as advantages. Yes, payments could go higher, a lot higher. But, if you happen to get the mortgage at the top of an interest-rate cycle, they could also fall, significantly. As we go through this chapter, we'll talk more about the pros and cons of the ARM, but first let's get a better idea of the specifics of this type of mortgage.

BANK ARMs VERSUS S&L ARMs

The federal governing bodies for banks and savings and loan associations have both allowed their member institutions to issue ARMs, so these mortgages are widely available nationwide. However, the specific regulations with regard to banks and S&Ls are different in some important areas. Since the largest source of mortgage money has traditionally been the S&L, we'll consider the S&L ARM. But, along the way, the differences between it and the bank ARMs will be indicated.

MAXIMUM LOAN AMOUNT

Generally speaking, ARMs can be issued for any mortgage amount that the lender is authorized to loan. Different lenders have different amounts. Some banks can go into the hundreds of thousands of dollars. Some savings and loans are limited to smaller mortgages. In general, however, the maximum mortgage amount is often a factor of the conditions of the secondary market.

As of this writing, ARMs are being accepted by the Federal National Mortgage Association (Fannie Mae) in all of the forms we'll discuss in this chapter. They are also accepted by the Federal Home Loan Mortgage Corporation (Freddie Mac—another secondary lender), but without negative amortization (which we'll explain in a moment).

MINIMUM DOWN PAYMENT

The down payment on an ARM is roughly the same as it was for the old fixed-rate mortgages. Generally, the mortgages require 20 percent down. However, with mortgage insurance (see the chapter on PMIs) a down payment of as little as 10 or even 5 percent may be allowed. Again, it depends on the lender.

INTEREST-RATE ADJUSTMENT AND LIMITING MONTHLY PAYMENTS

As Peter and Helga found out, the nature of an ARM is that the interest rate may move up and down. This has some potentially disastrous consequences for the borrower. For example, what if you take out a mortgage at 12 percent interest and 1 year later the mortgage rate doubles to 24 percent?

Admittedly, this is an extreme example. But, I think it does illustrate one of the great dangers of an ARM—namely that monthly payments could rise far faster than the ability of the buyer to pay for the rises.

How can a borrower accept a mortgage with so unlimited a kind of monthly payment?

The lender's approach to this initially was that it couldn't be helped. After all, the lender has to live in a world where it's paying adjustable interest on deposits. By 1980, 43 percent of all bank deposits and 58 pecent of all savings and loan association deposits were interest-rate–sensitive. It has been estimated that, with deregulation in the banking industry, by 1985, 100 percent of all deposits with both lenders will be interest-rate–sensitive. There is no way that such a lender can, on the one hand, offer an adjustable rate to depositors and a fixed rate to borrowers. The fixed rate, in this circumstance, has to go.

But, though this argument may be true, it holds out little help to the borrower. When a drowning person yells for help, you can carefully explain that you don't have a life preserver to throw to him or her. But, that doesn't help the person stay afloat. You have to look for something else to throw.

That's what the lenders have done. They've looked for other ways of insulating the borrower from too-rapid rises in the mortgage interest rate. They have come up with a number of solutions.

Extending the Mortgage Period

The first solution was to extend the period of the mortgages. Normally, ARMs are made for 30 years. Savings and loan associations are allowed to extend that period of the mortgage for up to 40 years (banks are not). Extending the mortgage will help the borrower. A longer term means a lower monthly payback. But, as we saw in the chapter on fixed-interest-rate mortgages, going from 30 to 40 years does not help that much. A single increase of only ½ percent wipes out the advantages gained by increasing the loan for 10 years.

Another method of keeping the monthly payment low on the ARM is called "capping."

Capping the ARM

"Capping" means that the lender agrees in the mortgage contract that at no point in time will the monthly payment be increased above a certain stipulated percentage in any one year. This capping the potential rise of the monthly payment is a kind of stabilizing guarantee to the borrower. The borrower at least knows the parameters of the mortgage payment this way and can budget accordingly. Instead of worrying about the payment potentially doubling by one year's end, the borrower knows, for example, that under no circumstances would the monthly payment go up by more than, for example, 5 percent. To clarify: The "cap" applies to increases in monthly payment—not increases in interest rate. A 5-percent cap means the monthly payment cannot increase more than 5 percent over a year, regardless of what the interest rate does. For example, if the monthly payment were $100 at 5-percent cap, it could not go higher than $105. The interest rate during the same period could double. The capped monthly rate would still be limited to the 5-percent increase. This knowledge is worth a great deal of peace at mind, especially when trying to sleep at night.

Here are the effects of capping the monthly payment on a 30-year, $50,000 mortgage with an initial interest rate of 12 percent (Table 4-1). I've arbitrarily picked four cap rates—5 percent, 7½ percent, 10 percent, and no cap at all. Interest rates are based on interest-rate jumps during the volatile period of 1978 to 1981.

TABLE 4–1. "CAP" RATE COMPARISON CHART. (30-year, $50,000 mortgage, initial interest rate—12 percent)

		Monthly payment ($)				***Remaining balance ($)***			
Year	***Rate (%)***	***5% Cap***	***7.5% Cap***	***10% Cap***	***No Cap***	***5% Cap***	***7.5 Cap***	***10% Cap***	***No Cap***
1	12	514	514	514	514	49,818	49,818	49,818	49,818
2	13.5	540	552	565	572	50,079	49,915	49,751	49,669
3	15	567	594	622	630	50,837	50,295	49,745	49,544
4	16.5	595	638	684	689	52,180	50,977	49,738	49,437
5	18	625	686	753	748	54,235	51,992	49,648	49,344
6	"	656	738	"	"	56,284	52,534	49,535	49,231
10	"	797	800	"	"	63,908	51,838	48,815	48,516
15	"	1018	"	"	"	68,591	49,678	46,781	46,494
20	"	1112	"	"	"	61,723	44,400	41,811	41,555
25	"	"	"	"	"	43,797	31,505	29,668	29,486
29	"	"	"	"	"	12,130	8,726	8,217	8,167

Note: For purposes of this illustration, the interest rate is presumed to fluctuate only until year five, after which it remains constant for the term of the loan. In actual practice, this is only the case with bank ARMs, not S&L ARMs, as we'll see later.

Source: J. J. Finn, *The Federal Home Loan Bank Board,* February 27, 1981.

Note how the monthly payment fluctuates during the payback period. The lowest cap rate, 5 percent, shows low annual increases. But, those increases continue for 20 years until a stable payback rate of over twice the initial payment is achieved.

On the other hand, a higher cap rate, one in which the monthly payment is allowed to increase by as much as 10 percent annually, stabilizes right along with the interest rate. That is, the monthly payment is able to rise to accommodate the rise in interest rates. Although the *initial* rise is higher, the *ultimate* rise is only to just under 50 percent of the original monthly payment by year five.

The important point to grasp here (it's very important because it must be understood to grasp our next concept) is that when interest rates go up, there's more interest to be paid on the money borrowed. If the amount borrowed is $50,000 and the interest rate is 10 percent, the annual interest that *must be paid* is $5000. If the interest rate on the $50,000 is 20 percent, that's $10,000 interest that *must be paid.* Either way, there is no possibility of avoiding the interest. Regardless of the cap on the mortgage, the interest *must be paid.*

Hypothetical $50,000 mortgage at two interest rates

$50,000		$50,000
× 10%	Interest rate	× 20%
$5,000	Annual interest that *must be paid*	$10,000
$450	Monthly payment	$450

Putting a cap on the monthly payment does not mean that the amount of interest that *must be paid* is somehow avoided, overlooked, or forgiven. The interest is still there. Putting the cap on the monthly payment only means that the interest which is due may be paid back in the future instead of in the present. This has interesting consequences for the borower.

NEGATIVE AMORTIZATION

Go back to Table 4-1 and look down the remaining balance column for a 5-percent cap rate to year fifteen. Note the amount. It is $68,591. That is the balance owed the lender after 15 years. Now look up to the top of the chart to see how much was initially borrowed. It was $50,000. By putting a low cap rate on the monthly payment, the interest which must be paid is deferred to the future. That is, the interest is *accrued*. It is added to the mortgage amount and it becomes principal on which new interest must be paid. It's interest on interest! In our example, by year fifteen with a 5-percent cap rate, the borrower owes $18,591 *more* than he or she originally borrowed. That's a 37 percent increase in the amount of the mortgage.

Amount owed at year fifteen	$ 68,591
Amount originally borrowed	– 50,000
Increase in principal	$ 18,591

Ending up owing more than you borrow through interest accrual (paying interest on interest) is called "negative amortization."

Instead of the monthly payment being large enough to pay off the mortgage, the monthly payment is too small. Instead of paying off the mortgage, it builds the mortgage up. And, since the effect is compounded, the borrower ends up paying interest on accrued interest. The effect can be devastating. And usually it's all to save just a very few dollars at the beginning. Consider the two monthly payments—one with a cap rate of 5 percent, the other with 10 percent. The 5 percent cap rate accrues interest—the 10 percent rate is high enough not to.

Year	5% Cap Monthly payment ($)	10% Cap Monthly payment ($)	Difference ($)
1	514	514	0
2	540	565	25
3	567	622	55
4	638	684	46
5	625	753	128
6	656	753	97
20	1112	753	– 359

Notice the "difference" column. In this one example, for the first 3 years, the difference in monthly payments is actually around $50 or less. For the next 2 years, it is around $100. But, by the time we get to the twentieth year of the mortgage, it's actually reversed. The person with the 10-percent cap rate is paying $359 per month *less* than the person with the 5-percent cap rate.

Negative amortization occurs only when the borrower is unable or does not want to make a monthly payment sufficiently high to pay back the money borrowed plus interest. My own feeling is that, since the difference between being able to fully pay back and having to negatively amortize is usually only a few dollars, it's worth the strain to pay back fully. Paying interest on interest (which is what happens in negative amortization) is, in my opinion, the worst kind of folly.*

Lenders, however, have another way of looking at the accrued interest of negative amortization. Although the present tax laws prevent them from calling it anything but interest, they prefer to think of it as a kind of shared capital. They point out that interest rates follow inflation. When inflation goes up, so do interest rates. And, they further conclude, that housing prices follow inflation. (This is not necessarily so because high interest rates tend to *deflate* housing prices, as we saw earlier.)

Therefore, the conclusion is drawn, a negatively amortized mortgage is a way of sharing in the price appreciation of the house. The lender here is simply sharing in the potential appreciation (profit) of the property.

Negative Amortization from the Borrower's Viewpoint

For the borrower, this way of looking at things makes for a crucial decision at the time of borrowing. To a great extent, deciding on whether or not to get an ARM depends on whether or not your property is going to appreciate. For example, if you buy a home on which the mortgage goes up $18,000 over 5 years, but the price of the home goes up $50,000, you're not going to complain too loudly. You may have made less, but you've still made something.

On the other hand, if the price of the home doesn't go up at all during 5 years, then you may want to scream. The $18,000 the mortgage went up comes right out of your equity in the property—the amount you put down.

---

* Banks are required to adjust payments every 5 years to fully amortize the remaining balance of the mortgage.

Profit vs. ARM

$120,000 property with $100,000 ARM
$18,000 negative amortization after 5 years.

$120,000	Resale value	$170,000	
– 118,000	Mortgage	– 118,000	
2,000	Equity	52,000	
– 20,000	Original down payment	– 20,000	
– $ 18,000	Loss with low appreciation	$ 32,000	Profit with high appreciation

If the property appreciates, you make money—in this case, $32,000 over and above the money you originally put in. But, if the property should remain static in price—be worth just the same as what you bought it for— you lose your down payment!

Of course, who expects a house anywhere in the country to remain static in price over the next 5 years?

Actually, prices will probably advance on all fronts, but not equally as fast. In the real world, negative amortization could truly be a problem if you've bought in a low-demand, low-appreciation area. It could indeed cost you a loss of money.

Limits on Negative Amortization

Savings and loan regulations provide for unlimited negative amortization. They can, if they want, keep a steady payment and keep adding the interest accrued to the principal almost indefinitely.

Banks, on the other hand, have strict limits on negative amortization in mortgages. The rule reads, "The amount of negative amortization, if any, permitted during any period (adjustment period minimum is 6 months) may not exceed 1.0 percent of the principal outstanding at the beginning of that period multiplied by the number of whole consecutive 6-month periods included in the interval between payment changes. In no event may the amount of negative amortization allowed under the preceding sentence exceed 10 percent of the principal outstanding at the beginning of the period."

Regardless of whether or not the lenders are permitted to use negative amortization through the use of monthly payment caps, whether they do use it may depend on something totally different. It may depend on what lenders in the secondary market are willing to accept.

As of this writing, Freddie Mac (Federal Home Loan Mortgage Corporation) has indicated it will not accept *any* negative amortization. That means that if a lender wants to use the capping procedure, it will have to do so only with those mortgages it intends keeping strictly for its own portfolio. (Or sell to Fannie Mae.)

VOLUNTARY INTEREST-RATE LIMITATIONS

The final method of limiting monthly payments is for the lender to voluntarily limit changes in the interest rate.

Although the new laws may permit unlimited interest-rate adjustments for savings and loan associations, these associations do not have to insist on using them. They can *voluntarily* limit such interest rate movements to, for example, 2 percent per year. (Banks are already limited to a 2 percent per-year movement.)

At first, it may seem unlikely that all S&Ls would do this. However, there are good reasons for it. The savings and loan association wants to lend money on which it can collect interest. It does not want to force homeowners into foreclosure and acquire overpriced property. (Remember, the mortgage value could go up through negative amortization faster than the house appreciated.) Therefore, an association which insists on an unreasonable interest rate may find that:

1. Few borrowers want its mortgages.
2. Those that take them are often forced into foreclosure.
3. Bad publicity from its practices are forcing it out of business.

We may soon see a time when associations (and banks) advertise their terms just as they now advertise their interest rates. One may allow only a maximum interest-rate hike of 3 percent, another of 1½ percent. The borrower will shop around for the best combination of terms and interest rates. Here are some of the other terms of importance.

ADJUSTMENT PERIODS

The minimum adjustment period for an ARM is 6 months. But, that is not the maximum period. The maximum can vary greatly but, in most cases, it will not be more than 1 year.

In general, a lender must notify the borrower of a change in the adjustment period not less than 30 nor more than 45 days before the adjustment. *There can be no costs, fees, or expenses of any kind to the borrower for the change in interest rate at the adjustment period.*

(The reason for the notification period is so that, in theory, the borrower could go out and search for another mortgage. However, since ARMs very likely will be the only game in town, there are few other places a borrower can hop to.)

INDICES

The interest rate on the ARM, as noted earlier, is tied to an index. When the index moves up, the interest rate on the monthly payment moves up. When the index moves down, so should the interest on that payment.*

Choosing the right index, therefore, can have a lot to say about how much the monthly payments jump around.

This leads to an interesting story that occurred in Florida in the mid-1970s. At that time, condominiums were all the rage. When the developers sold them, however, they kept at least one string attached. The developers said, in effect, that the buyers really didn't know anything about running the recreational facilities. They didn't know about swimming pool maintenance, golf course maintenance, tennis court maintenance, and so forth. For what started as a nominal fee,

---

* Lenders may or may not actually raise the interest according to their preference. But, they *must* lower it if the index goes down.

the developer would handle these facilities on an ongoing basis.

But, what many developers did was to attach their fee to an index. They chose the Consumer Price Index.

When inflation soared, the index soared and so did the fee the condo owners were paying to the developers. In many cases, after a few years, the fee for recreational facilities became higher than the homeowner's entire costs for principal, interest, taxes, and insurance on the condo!

Needless to say, something had to be done, and it took court cases and legislative relief to alleviate the problem.

The same, potentially, could happen to the ARMs. If they were tied to the CPI, they too could soar through the roof. Therefore, knowing what index your ARM is tied to is important.

The Federal Home Loan Bank Board has given the savings and loans a wide choice in the index they select. Generally, it may be ". . . any interest rate index that is readily verifiable by the borrower and that is beyond the control of the lender." (This, at least, prevents the lender from using its own mortgage rates as the index—it prevents them from arbitrarily raising or lowering the ARM interest rates.)

The Comptroller of the Currency, however, was much more specific in the indices that banks could choose on which to base their ARMs. The banks must choose one of the following three:

1. The monthly average contract interest rate charged by all lenders on mortgage loans for previously occupied homes. This is found in the Federal Home Loan Bank Board's journal and is usually available by the twelfth of each month.

2. The monthly average yield on U.S. Treasury securities adjusted to a constant maturity of 3 years. This can be found in the *Federal Reserve Bulletin*. It's usually available the first week of each month.

3. The monthly average of weekly average auction rates on U.S. Treasury bills with a maturity of 6 months, again as found in the *Federal Reserve Bulletin*.

Since the Federal Home Loan Bank Board advised (but did not insist) its member savings and loan associations also use these indices, it is likely they are the ones which will be used. Table 4-2 is a comparison of the three indices given in 6-month intervals between 1969 and 1980.

TABLE 4–2. HOW THREE INDEXES WHICH COULD BE USED FOR ADJUSTABLE RATE MORTGAGES HAVE FLUCTUATED IN THE PAST.
(Monthly Rate for June and December 1969–1980, %)

	Mortgage rates on previously occupied homes[1]	***3-year Treasury rates***[2]	***6-month Treasury rates***[3]
1969: June	7.64	6.83	6.725
December	8.08	18.10	7.788
1970: June	8.19	7.84	6.907
December	4.12	5.75	4.848
1971: June	7.38	6.32	4.890
December	7.51	6.27	4.199
1972: June	7.36	5.64	4.270
December	7.45	6.01	5.287
1973: June	7.64	6.83	7.234
December	8.46	6.81	7.444
1974: June	8.66	8.15	8.232
December	9.39	7.24	7.091
1975: June	8.86	7.17	5.463
December	9.09	7.43	5.933
1976: June	8.82	7.32	5.784
December	8.90	5.68	4.513
1977: June	8.78	6.39	5.198
December	6.93	7.30	6.377
1978: June	9.27	8.60	7.290
December	9.85	9.53	9.079
1979: June	10.16	8.95	9.062
December	11.50	10.71	11.547
1980: June	12.98	8.91	7.216
December	13.15	13.65	14.770

[1]The average contract interest rate charged by all lenders on mortgage loans for previously occupied homes as published by the Federal Home Loan Bank Board in monthly news releases and in its *Journal*.

[2]The average monthly yield on the U.S. Treasury securities adjusted to a constant maturity of 3 years based on daily closing bid prices as published monthly in Federal Reserve Board Statistical Release G. 13(415) and in the *Federal Reserve Bulletin*.

[3]The monthly average of weekly average auction rates on U.S. Treasury bills with a maturity of 6 months as published monthly in Federal Reserve Board Statistical Release G. 13(415) and in the *Federal Reserve Bulletin*.

Please note in looking at these indices that these are not the interest rates which would be charged. Rather, the interest rates charged on an ARM would be based on a *movement* in the indices.

Also, compare the first (mortgage rates on previously occupied homes) with the remaining two. Note that, since the mortgage rate reflects the actual cost of mortgage money, its changes during the more volatile years of 1979 and 1980 were much lower than for the other two indices. Three-year Treasury-bill rates, for example, moved from 8.91 percent to 13.65 percent in 1980 alone. Six-month T-bill rates moved from 7.2 percent to 14.8 percent! The latter was a more than doubling of the interest rate in only 1 year.

Consider a borrower who had obtained a mortgage in June of 1980, using the 6-month Treasury rate. By December, the index having doubled would mean that the interest rate on that person's mortgage could double! If the initial interest rate was 14 percent, it would now be 28 percent!

Of course, banks, (not S&Ls) can't increase interest more than 2 percent a year on their mortgages. But, they are allowed to carry over uncharged interest-rate hikes.

Savings and loans, however, have no such rule restrictions. If our borrower had an ARM tied to the 6-month T-bill rate with no caps on interest (or monthly payment), then within 6 months of obtaining the mortgage, that person's payments would indeed have doubled.

Get the Best Index for You

Does that mean it's better not to go to a lender who relies on the T-bill rates?

Not necessarily, but it is something to think about. If I were getting an ARM mortgage, I would want it *tied to the least volatile* interest rate. According to the above chart, for the period of 1969 to 1980, that would be the first column, or previously occupied home mortgage rates.

I wouldn't want it tied to the highly volatile 6-month T-bill rate.

On the other hand, if I were a savings and loan, I would want the index tied to the interest rate that most reflected my actual cost of money in the short-term market. Of the three, that might very well be the 6-month Treasury-bill rate.

Of course, there's no guarantee that future rate changes will occur in the same manner as those have in the past. It may turn out that, as more and more ARMs get on the books, the first columns (mortgage rates) may become more volatile.

PREPAYMENT

Can a borrower prepay an ARM as soon as he or she wants? This question may come into play when someone is intent on buying a property and then quickly reselling it.

The answer is yes and no. To prevent borrowers from quickly changing over their ARMs, both the savings and loans and the banks may prohibit prepayment (or charge a fee for it) if it occurs prior to the first adjustment period. (Remember, adjustment periods are for a minimum of 6 months.)

Within 30 days of the adjustment period, however, prepayment is allowed. That was one of the conditions of the adjustment—the borrower was notified 30 days in advance so he or she could then shop around looking for a new mortgage. Generally, after the first interest-rate adjustment period, prepayment is allowed without a penalty.

ASSUMPTION OF MORTGAGE

Can the ARM be assumed by someone upon sale of the property? While at first the logical answer might seem yes, the true answer is no.

It would seem that there is no particular advantage to the lender in preventing assumption. Since the mortgage interest rate on an ARM fluctuates up and down with market conditions, the mortgage should always be fairly well in line with short-term money costs. And since the major reason for preventing assumptions was to force the borrower to turn in the mortgage so a new one at competitive rates could be obtained, why prohibit assumption?

Why indeed? Yet, both the Federal Home Loan Bank Board and the Comptroller of Currency have indicated that lenders may insert due-on clauses. (These mean that, upon sale of the property, the exisitng ARM will have to be paid off.) The reasons given were that this simply was another bit of protection for the lender. It certainly is, but it does nothing to help the consumer.

MAXIMUM LATE CHARGE

One final little bit of information concerns how much of a late charge the lender may have on the mortgage. This is the charge assessed if the monthly payment is more than 15 days late, yet not late enough to be placed into default.

Freddie Mac has a provision on mortgages it buys which has become a kind of standard. The maximum late charge for its mortgage is 5 percent of the monthly payment.

ADVANTAGES OF ARMs

From the buyer's viewpoint, I can see only two advantages to the ARM. The first advantage is simply that there will be a mortgage available when there otherwise might not be one. In other words, if you have no other choice, take an ARM.

The second advantage is that there is often a lower *initial* interest rate on the ARM.

Lower Initial Interest Rate on the ARM

The reason that many lenders are able to offer a lower initial interest rate on the ARM than on a fixed-rate mortgage (as much as 2 or 3 percent lower!) is that they don't have to outguess the market on the ARM.

On a fixed-rate mortgage, the lender in the recent past had to contend with sharp increases in the cost of money. Therefore, to compensate, the lender often charged 2 or 3 percent higher than necessary at the origination of the mortgage. The idea was that, even if the short-term rates shot up, the lender would at least be partially covered.

Under the ARM, however, since the interest rate is fully adjustable, the lender no longer has to insist on this cushion and can offer a realistic interest rate.

DISADVANTAGES OF THE ARMs

The disadvantages of the ARMs could fill a book this size. Yet, I'm not trying to be discouraging. Although these are vastly inferior mortgages from a consumer's viewpoint than the old fixed-rate mortgage, as noted above, they are still better than nothing. And if you, as borrower, are careful, you can avoid many of the pitfalls.

1. No set monthly payment—This is the single worst feature of an ARM. Without knowing for sure what your monthly payment is going to be, it becomes almost impossible to plan a budget. How can a couple, for example, know what to spend on food, on clothing , on recreation, on gas, and so on, if their mortgage payment can fluctuate several hundred dollars per year? Should they save money now anticipating a big hike later on? Or should they spend up to the hilt and hope for the best?

Unfortunatly, most of us are in a situation in which we are already spending up to the hilt. Big and sudden (30 days notice is hardly a long time to be made aware) changes could devastate our financing. We could be forced to sell or refinance or lose the property.

The truth of the matter is that borrowers simply aren't in as good a position to adjust their monthly payments significantly. On the other hand, the large lending institutions are in a better position to rearrange their financing. They have accountants, attorneys, and economists on staff. By any sense of fairness, it should be the lenders who have the major burden of fluctuating interest rates, not the borrowers.

Of course, in the past, with the fixed-rate mortgage, the borrowers had none of this burden and the lenders had all. What we see in the ARM is a swing of the pendulum too far in the other direction. What we see is an overprotection of the lender at the expense of the borrower.

But, the market place has a way of dealing with inequities. If lenders offer unreasonable terms on their ARMs (no limits on interest-rate fluctuations), then they won't find borrowers flocking to their doors. And those borrowers they do get often will be unable to qualify. Regardless of what they may be allowed to do, I suspect that within a year or so most lenders will *voluntarily* be offering restrictions on their ARMs. They will be in competition with other lenders and they will be seeking to allure borrowers. Consequently, they will have to offer better terms.

2. A second disadvantage of the ARM is its complexity. In the last few chapters, we've discussed fixed-rate mortgages and SAMs. While much of our discussion related to the pros and cons, the actual explanation of how the mortgage worked was fairly straightforward and short. Here, with the ARM, I've felt compelled to go on at length in order to fully explain the mortgage. Even now, I am not sure that I've sufficiently covered all the details to make it understandable to a totally lay reader.

The problem with the ARM is that it is sophiscated. And the decision as to which ARM to get requires sophisticated judgment. In the old days, it was simply a matter of comparing the interest rates. The government, in the early 1970s, even came up with a method of making this comparison easier, using the annual percentage rate (APR), which could be standardized and used by all lenders. This made comparison shopping easy for consumers.

But, what is a borrower to do with an ARM? Does it have negative amortization or not? Is that good or bad? What index does it use and what does that mean for the mortgage? Is it capped or not? And so forth.

To help readers examine ARMs which they have been considering, I've prepared the following comparison sheet. While it by no means looks at all the possible areas of concern, it does cover many of the more important ones.

ARM COMPARISON SHEET

	Mortgage #1	***Mortgage #2***	***Mortgage #3***
Initial monthly payments?	________	________	________
Initial interest rate?	________	________	________
Adjustment period occurs every____ months	________	________	________

(Note: A long adjustment period is usually to the advantage of the borrower.)

Limit if any on *interest* change per adjustment period?	________	________	________
Limit, if any, on monthly payment (capping)?	________	________	________
Does negative amortization occur?	Yes/No?	Yes/No?	Yes/No?
Limit, if any, on maximum negative amortization?	________	________	________

Does mortgage fully amortize after a certain date?	Yes/No?	Yes/No?	Yes/No?
How many years from now does mortgage fully amortize?	________	________	________
Name of index used for adjustment?	________	________	________
Does lender offer a detail showing how payments would have changed on this loan given the index over the previous 5 years?	Yes/No?	Yes/No? (If not, go see another lender!)	Yes/No?
Is index highly volatile or steady?	________	________	________

This is my basic questionnaire for anyone considering an ARM. Once this questionnaire is filled out, the potential borrower should have an idea of what he or she is getting into.

Now, I suggest a further checksheet. This one will help determine if you can afford to get the ARM you are considering.

ARM DECISION SHEET

Given what you know about the ARMs you may be considering, what is the *maximum* each is likely to fluctuate per adjustment period over the next few years? (You can also factor into here your own assessment of the economy.)

Mortgage #1 ________ #2 ________ #3 ________

Cut the above amounts in half and assume that this will *be the average* fluctuation per period. *Can your income and budget survive this amount of an increase every adjustment period* (probably every 6 months)?

Mortgage #1 ________ #2 ________ #3 ________

By cutting the amount in half, we're assuming that some adjustment periods will be zero while others will be the maximum. In actual practice, some adjustment periods may see the mortgage interest rate *decline.* Of course, in that eventuality, there would be no problem whatsoever for you. But, for safety, I believe the borrower should be prepared for increases. If there's anything that the past 5 years have taught us, it's that there's no real way to predict what's going to happen to interest rates in this economy.

Given what you know about the ARMs you may be considering, do you understand what it means if your ARM has *negative amortization*? (If not, try rereading pages 54–58.)

If you understand it, what is the maximum amount of negative amortization likely to occur during the first 5 years of your ARM?

Mortgage #1 __________ #2 __________ #3 __________

Will the price of your property appreciate sufficiently to warrant this type of negative amortization? (Remember, if the price doesn't go up, then the accrued interest comes first out of the money you put into the property as a down payment!)

My final question is this: Isn't there some way you can get a different kind of mortgage?

To help borrowers understand the nature of ARMs and some of the dangers involved, both the Comptroller of the Currency for banks and the Federal Home Loan Bank Board for savings and loans has insisted that all borrowers receive a disclosure statement. This statement helps to describe the ARM and many of its conditions. To help you understand the ARM, you'll find below the model disclosure statement suggested by the Federal Home Loan Bank Board for its adjustable-rate mortgage. (Please note that the FHLBB used the term adjustable-mortgage loan, or AML, in its description.)

IMPORTANT INFORMATION ABOUT THE ADJUSTABLE MORTGAGE LOAN—PLEASE READ CAREFULLY

You have received an application form for an adjustable mortgage loan (AML). The AML may differ from other mortgages with which you are familiar.

General Description of Adjustable Mortgage Loan

The adjustable mortgage loan is a flexible loan instrument. Its interest rate may be adjusted by the lender from time to time. Such adjustments will result in increases or decreases in your payment amount, in the outstanding principal loan balance, in the loan term, or in all three (see discussion below relating to these types of adjustments). Federal regulations place no limit on the amount by which the interest rate may be adjusted either at any one time or over the life of the loan, or on the frequency with which it may be adjusted. Adjustments to the interest rate must reflect the movement of a single, specified index (see discussion below). This does not mean that the particular loan agreement you sign must, by law, permit unlimited interest-rate changes. It merely means that, if you desire to have certain rate adjustment limitations placed in your loan agreement, that is a matter you should negotiate with the lender. You may also want to make inquiries concerning the loan terms offered by other lenders on AMLs to compare the terms and conditions.

Another flexible feature of the AML is that the regular payment amount may be increased or decreased by the lender from time to time to reflect changes in the interest rate. Again, federal regulations place no limitations on the amount by which the lender may adjust payments at any one time, or on the frequency of payment adjustments. If you wish to have particular provisions in your loan agreement regarding adjustments to the payment amount, you should negotiate such terms with the lender.

A third flexible feature of the AML is that the outstanding principal loan balance (the total amount you owe) may be increased or decreased from time to time when, because of adjustments to the interest rate, the payment amount is either too small to cover interest due on the loan, or larger than is necessary to pay off the loan over the remaining term of the loan.

The final flexible feature of the AML is that the loan term may be lengthened or shortened from time to time, corresponding to an increase or decrease in the interest rate. When the term is extended in connection with a rate increase, the payment amount does not have to be increased to the same extent as if the term had not been lengthened. In no case may the total term of the loan exceed 40 years.

The combination of these four basic features allows an association to offer a variety of mortgage loans. For example, one type of loan could permit rate adjustments with corresponding changes in the payment amount. Alternatively, a loan could permit rate adjustments to occur more frequently than payment adjustments, limit the amount by which the payment could be adjusted, and/or provide for corresponding adjustments to the principal loan balance.

Key terms of ____________________ Federal Savings and Loan Association's adjustable mortgage loan

Following is a summary of the basic terms on the type of AML to be offered to you. This summary is intended for reference purposes only.

Important information relating specifically to your loan will be contained in the loan agreement.

[Provide summary of basic terms of the loan, including the loan term, the frequency of rate changes, the frequency of payment changes, the maximum rate change, if any, at one time, the maximum rate change, if any, over the life of the loan, the maximum payment change, if any, at one time, minimum increments, if any, of rate changes, and whether there will be adjustments to the principal loan balance, in the following format:

Loan term ....
Frequency of rate changes ....
Frequency of payment changes ....]

How Your Adjustable Mortgage Loan Would Work

Initial interest rate

The initial interest rate offered by __________ Federal Savings and Loan Association on your AML will be established and disclosed to you on [commitment date, etc.] based on market conditions at the time.

Notice of payment adjustments

__________ Federal Savings and Loan Association will send you notice of an adjustment to the payment amount at least 30 but not more than 45 days before it becomes effective.

Fees

You will be charged fees by __________ Federal Savings and Loan Association and by other persons in connection with the origination of your AML. The association will give you an estimate of these fees after receiving your loan application.

BALLOON PAYMENT OR "BULLET" MORTGAGES

Thus far we have been speaking of adjustable-rate mortgages which are fully amortized—that is, the entire amount borrowed plus interest is paid off at the end of the mortgage term.

A different kind of ARM is available, however, and it is beginning to see increased use. At some point in the future many in the industry predict it could become the standard. It is the "balloon payment" adjustable rate or, as it is sometimes referred to in the industry, the "bullet" mortgage.

What makes the balloon payment mortgage different is that it is not fully paid off. Rather, it has a set termination date which can be anywhere from a few years to 15 or 20 years. The point is that when this loan comes due, the property will not have been fully paid clear. There will be a large last payment—sometimes very large.

Its actual operation is very simple. In many cases the borrower will find that the form of the mortgage is identical to that of the ARM. Monthly payments will include principal and interest, and the loan will be written to amortize fully. In fact, if the borrower were allowed to keep paying over the term, the money would be fully repaid.

However, the borrower is not allowed that option under this type of mortgage. Rather, a date, perhaps 10 years, is arbitrarily fixed. At that point the mortgage must be repaid in full.

If you'll recall our discussion in the fixed-rate mortgage chapters, we noted that very little of the principal is normally paid off by year ten (on a 30-year amortization term). The result of a balloon payment is that frequently after paying for 10 years the borrower could find that he or she owes as much as was originally borrowed.

In the case of adjustable-rate mortgages with negative amortization, the borrower could end up suddenly having a balloon payment for more than the amount originally borrowed!

To protect against this, savings and loan associations may not increase interest beyond an amount which can be accommodated by extending the maturity of the loan to 40 years, *if the mortgage is on an owner-occupied dwelling.* (If it's on other types of property, no such protection is offered.)

The advantage to the lender of the balloon-payment mortgage is that the money can be recalled at a specific time—often only 5 or 7 years out. That protects the lender against unforeseen changes in the market. In a sense, giving such a loan, from a lender's viewpoint, is like shooting a bullet. It penetrates a certain distance and then stops. It doesn't keep going on and on for 30 or 40 years. Hence the nickname, "bullet" mortgage.

For the borrower it would seem there are only disadvantages. At least with the standard adjustable-rate mortgage, given all its other drawbacks, there was the comfort of knowing that if the property were held for 30 or 40 years, the mortgage could indeed be fully paid back. Now even that security is gone. You might need to refinance in only 5 years, even with a mortgage from a savings and loan association!

Hidden in all this, however, there is one advantage. The lender may not dramatically increase the interest rate if you're an owner-occupant. In fact, in some cases (a 30-year amortization period with a shorter balloon) the lender probably wouldn't be able to increase the interest rate beyond ½ percent or so! (However, for a shorter amortization term, say 15 years with a 5-year balloon, the increase could be much, much higher.)

The ultimate result of the balloon payment is to give lenders more flexibility in calling in their money and adjusting it to changing interest rates. For the borrower it means even more sophisticated financing and less long-term security.

It's hard for me to visualize the housing industry in this country getting to where it is today if we had had only ARMs in the past. I believe that more likely we would have ended up with fewer houses built, far fewer, and of much poorer quality.

It is also hard for me to visualize that the unrestricted ARMs will be widely accepted by borrowers. The risks to the borrowers are simply too great. (Of course, if the buyer gets the house at the top of an interest-rate cycle, he or she can ride the monthly payment down. But, what if the home is purchased at the bottom of a cycle?)

While it's not necessarily the case that the only good ARM is somebody else's ARM, it may be true that the borrower of tomorrow will be able to obtain a voluntarily restricted ARM, one that is something between the unrestricted ARMs allowed by the regulatory agencies and the old fixed-rate mortgages.

My one last plug here is for the mortgage banker. (I am not one myself nor do I have any association with them.) I believe that, in the future, they are the people the borrowers will go to when it's time to obtain a mortgage. The mortgage banker will have access to all the different kinds of ARMs available. He or she will be able to match the borrower to the mortgage far better than individual savings and loans or banks can do with their own restricted portfolio.

In the future, to get a mortgage, we'll all have to become more sophisticated shoppers. And we'll all have to do a lot more shopping.

FIVE

Graduated Payment Mortgages—Cutting the First Years' Payments

Recent studies have indicated that well over 85 percent of home purchases in this country are made by people who already own a home. What this means is that most home buyers are, in reality, "moving up." They are simply exchanging one home for another, usually of higher value.

Past home buyers are able to do this because of two reasons. First, they are able to transfer their often sizable equities into the new property. This gives them a big down payment. Second, second-time homeowners frequently are individuals or families who are into their more productive years and have relatively high incomes. They can afford the high payments involved with buying a house today.

But, where does that leave the individual or young couple who is the first-time home buyer? How do they, often with limited incomes and little down payment, break into the housing market?

The answer that was specifically designed for them by the lending industry is the graduated payment mortgage (GPM). When combined with a low-down-payment feature, it offers reduced monthly payments in the early years of the mortgage. Then, presumably, as the borrower's income grows, it increases the monthly payments.

Low monthly payments when the buyer has a small income and then, gradually, higher monthly payments as the buyer's income increases. It's one method of solving the finance problem for housing.

HOW THE GPM WORKS

While the GPM's basic operation is quite simple to state—low payments at first, higher payments to make up for it later on—the actual operation of the mortgage is better seen from an example.

We'll take a variety of a GPM that's been around for a few years. It is the FHA-HUD plan. This particular mortgage was intended for use as part of an FHA loan. It incorporates the low-down-payment feature of the FHA with the reduced-payment feature of the GPM. The mortgage amount is for $35,000. The down payment on the property to obtain this mortgage was only $1250. Since this first example is taken from the mid 1970s, the interest rate is only 8½ percent for 30 years (Figure 5-1).*

The chart lists years from 1 through 11+. It also indicates level payment. The level payment is the same as fully amortizing the

	Level payment	GPM plans ($)				
Year+	**loan ($)**	**I**	**II**	**III**	**IV**	**V**
1	269	25	223	203	243	223
2	269	251	234	218	248	230
3	269	257	245	234	254	237
4	269	264	258	252	258	233
5	269	270	271	271	263	251
6	269	277	284	291	269	258
7	269	277	284	291	274	266
8	269	277	284	291	280	274
9	269	277	284	291	285	282
10	269	277	284	291	291	291
11+	269	277	284	291	297	300

FIGURE 5–1. Comparison of payment schedules of level-payment mortgage and GPM. (U.S. Department of Housing and Urban Development.) $35,000 loan—8½ percent interest, 30-year term. (From *How to Buy a Home at a Reasonable Price,* by Robert Irwin, Copyright © 1979 by McGraw-Hill. Used with permission of McGraw-Hill Book Company.)

* This same mortgage is still available today, although at current interest rates.

mortgage over a 30-year period. A payment of $269 per month will accomplish this.

Next to the level-payment loan are five separate GPM payment schedules. Each has different features.

Plan I—Cutting the Payments

This plan offers a rate of graduation of 2½ percent for a graduation term of 5 years. This simply means that the monthly payment increases *no more* than 2½ percent per month. If we were to take 2½ percent of the first year's monthly payment of $245, we would find it is approximately $6. We then add that $6 to the $245 and we get the second year's payment of $251.

$ 245	First year's payment
× .025	Rate of graduation
6	Increase after 1 year
+ 245	First year's payment
$ 251	Second year's payment

The graduation period is for 5 years. After that time, there is a level payment high enough to *fully amortize* the mortgage.

Under Plan I, note that the savings are not that substantial. At year one, the greatest year of savings, only $24 a month is saved under the plan.

The savings are listed below.

Year	Savings on monthly payment ($)
1	24
2	18
3	12
4	5
5	−1
6+	−8

Although there's a nominal savings initially, there is also a nominal loss in terms of higher monthly payments for the last 25 years of the mortgage.

This plan might be helpful for someone who was just trying to squeeze into a home and could barely make it.

Plan II—Cutting the Payments Lower

This plan takes the same term as Plan I, 5 years. But it doubles the graduation rate. It has a rate of 5 percent. Here's what the monthly savings now look like.

Year	Savings ($)
1	46
2	35
3	24
4	11
5	−3
6+	−15

Under Plan II, the savings, at least in the first 2 years of the mortgage, are substantial. In year one, the savings are 17 percent of the monthly payment.

In year two, they are 13 percent. That's enough to make a buyer stop and consider. If you can cut your payments by 17 percent the first year and 13 percent the second, maybe it's worthwhile having that extra heavy high payment for the last 25 years of the mortgage. After all, many buyers figure that, after 5 years, they will sell the property anyhow.

Plan III—a Radical Payment Reduction

This plan carries the whole process even further. With the same term, 5 years, it increases the graduation rate to 7½ percent. The results are dramatic:

7½ Percent GPM Rate

Year	Savings ($)
1	66
2	51
3	24
4	17
5	−2
6+	−22

The percent savings the first year here is about 25 percent. You can cut your monthly payments by one quarter under this plan. And they will stay lower than under a standard fixed-rate plan until year five. After year six, the payments will only be $22 higher than they would have been under a traditional mortgage.

It's easy to see why many people prefer this particular plan. They figure that by year five their income will have inceased significantly and inflation will have reduced the value of the dollar to the point where they can easily afford the higher payments later.

Plans IV and V—Increasing the Term

Plan IV goes back to a lower graduation rate—2 percent. But the term of the graduation period is extended for 10 years.

What should be apparent from this Plan IV is that extending the term works against the borrower more than it works for him or her. While it's true that, initially the monthly payment is marginally lower, ultimately it grows significantly higher. This plan is roughly comparable to Plan I. Yet Plan I which had a first-year's payment within $2 a month of this plan, ended up after year five with a monthly payment that was $14 lower than the final monthly payment on this plan.

All of which is not intended to confuse, but merely to once again illustrate that extending the life of the graduation, like extending the life of a mortgage, makes little difference in lowering the monthly payment after the first critical years.

Plan V is once again a 10-year term, this time with a 3 percent rate of graduation.

2 PERCENT GPM RATE—10-YEAR TERM

Year	Savings ($)
1	26
2	21
3	16
4	11
5	6
6	0
7	−5
8	−11
9	−16
10	−20
11+	−26

The FHA-HUD GPM plan has been in existence since about 1977. Other similar plans were adopted by the Federal Home Loan Bank Board for use by savings and loan associations in 1978 and 1979. However, at this writing, a new plan is in the process of adoption by the board which would radically change the GPM plan that we have been examining. It would allow much higher rates of graduation. And it would allow the GPM to be combined with an ARM, or adjustable-rate mortgage. (You'll recall we discussed ARMs in Chapter 4.)

COMBINING THE GPM WITH AN ADJUSTABLE-RATE MORTGAGE

The idea behind this new type of GPM is to acomplish two goals. The first is still to give the borrower a lower monthly payment. But, the second is to give the lender a rate of return that competes with short-term money markets.

However, when the adjustable-rate mortgage feature is added to the old-style GPM, strange things happen. To see this more clearly, let's consider a mortgage which is for $50,000 over 30 years with an initial interest rate of 13 percent.

This is a fairly standard type of mortgage, even with the adjustable-rate feature. Now, we'll add a few tricks. We'll say that:

1. This mortgage had a graduation period of 5 years. What this means is that, after 5 years, the mortgage should be fully amortized.

2. The *maximum* graduation rate is no longer 7.5 percent as it was in the past—but is 15 percent! (The actual graduation rate to be adopted could be even higher. It could be whatever amount is agreed upon between borrower and lender.)

3. Adjustments to the interest rate are permitted not every 6 months, as is the case with a standard adjustable-rate mortgage, but every 3 years. Adjustments are made based on an index, just as for the ARM.

Table 5-1 illustrates what we have if these conditions are added to a GPM.

TABLE 5–1. MORTGAGE BALANCE AND MONTHLY PAYMENT FOR A GPM/ ARM

Year	*Balance at end ($)*	*Rate ($)*	*Monthly payment ($)*	*Payment increase (%)*	*Cumulative increase (%)*
1	51,362.90	13	428.09	0	0
2	52,517.69	13	460.20	7.5	7.5
3	53,408.42	13	494.71	7.5	15.6
4	54,325.58	14.5	568.92	15	32.9
5	54,863.70	14.5	611.69	7.5	42.86
6	54.929.41	14.5	657.46	7.5	53.58
7	54,672.70	16	753.78	14.65	76.08
8	54,374.92	16	753.78	0	76.08
9	54,029.50	16	753.78	0	76.08
10	53,698.51	17.5	815.51	8.19	90.5

How the New GPM/ARM Works Over a Period of Time

The fixed-rate monthly payment on a $50,000 mortgage at 13 percent would be $553 per month. However, because of the high graduation rate and the GPM feature, the initial monthly payment is only $428 per month. That's a savings of $125 a month for the first year, or roughly 23 percent. Note that this is based on an initial graduation rate of 7.5 percent.

All goes well for the first 3 years with payments rising by 7.5 percent per year planning to level out after year five.

But, in year four, a big hike in interest rates occurs. In order to adjust for this hike, the monthly payments are increased to the maximum—15 percent over the previous year. By year five, we're back on target with a 7.5 percent increase over the previous year, and by year six, we've obtained a mortgage payment which would fully amortize the mortgage ($657.46) over the remaining 24 years of the mortgage term.

However, in year seven, we get a big new interest-rate hike from the index—from 14.5 percent to 16 percent. To compensate, the mortgage payment is raised. It does not quite have to go to the maximum 15 percent, but only to 14.65 percent to fully accept this raise. The payment remains level again until year ten, when another mortgage hike forces payments up. This time the payments rise 8.19 percent.

Don't be confused in this mortgage by the payment increases after year five. They are caused entirely by the *adjustable* interest-rate feature. The graduated payment feature phases out after year five with a stable monthly payment beginning in year six.

Features of the GPM/ARM

There are at least two features of this GPM/ARM mortgage which are noteworthy. The first is that the initial monthly payments are indeed significantly lower than they would have been with *either* a fixed-rate or a standard ARM mortgage. The graduated payment plan does indeed work in this sense.

Limiting the Negative Amortization

Secondly, note the second column indicating mortgage balance at the end of the year. In all of the first 10 years, the mortgage amount due is higher than originally borrowed! The automatic feature of this GPM/ARM is negative amortization. But, unlike the negative amortization we saw in the standard ARM, the negative amortization here is limited. If we assume the borrower put 15 percent down, the cash put into the property would have been roughly $7500.

$ 7,500	Down payment
+ 50,000	Mortgage
$ 57,500	Purchase price

At no time does the mortgage balance get over $55,000. The highest that it does get is at year six when it reaches $54,972. That roughly equals 95 percent of the initial purchase price of the initial value.

What I'm getting at here is that, in this particular GPM/ARM, the negative amortization never gets closer than 5 percent to the original value of the property. The debt never reaches or goes higher than the amount the borrower originally paid.

This is an important feature if you're a borrower and feel that your property may appreciate in value. You won't want to share that appreciation any more than you must with the lender.

Other features of this GPM are similar to those for the standard ARM mortgage. There is the opportunity to repay without penalty *after* the first interest-rate adjustment notice is sent.

And this mortgage is not assumable without the consent of the lender.

Finally, this is strictly an owner-occupant mortgage. This means that it is intended only for the person who intends to buy a home in which to live. The borrower must sign a statement that he or she intends to use the property as a residence, to occupy it and not rent it out for 6 months. Investors are not welcome to the GPM.

WHO BENEFITS MOST FROM A GPM?

As noted at the beginning and indicated by the discussion of the mortgage itself, the GPM is primarily designed for buyers who anticipate having increases in their income. (While the big eye-catching feature of this mortgage is the lower initial monthly payments, it must be remembered that the monthly payments increase each year until they are substantially higher than they would have been had this been a standard loan, either fixed-rate or ARM.)

Typically, the GPM works best for a young couple or an individual in the 25 to 35 age group. This is because advancement including increasing salary is usually fastest in this age group.

The GPM is not recommended for those on fixed incomes or for those whose incomes are likely to remain stable or decline. Typically, this means that the GPM would be a high-risk mortgage for the individual or family in the 50-plus age group.

ADVANTAGES OF THE GPM

The big advantage of the GPM has already been fairly well discussed—the lower initial payments. But, perhaps it's worth remembering that this lower monthly payment has an additional bonus. As you may recall when we discussed the SAMs, having a lower monthly payment gives the borrower two options.

First, for the same value of house price and mortgage, the monthly payment may be reduced, thus easing the burden on the borrower.

Second, instead of reducing the monthly payment, the use of a GPM may mean a borrower can get a higher mortgage and a higher-priced house. For example, let's say that we've been looking at homes in the $100,000 price range. We anticipate putting $10,000 down and will thus end up with a $90,000 mortgage. At 14 percent interest, our monthly payments will be $1066 plus taxes and insurance.

We're fairly well off financially and we figure we can just make the payments. Our lender agrees that we would qualify for the mortgage. Under the conventional approach, we would look for a home at no more than $100,000 in price.

But, now let's say that we can qualify for a GPM. Under the GPM, our initial first year's payment will still be roughly $1066. However, this represents a 25 percent reduction from the standard mortgage payment, because of the graduated feature. For $1066 at 14 percent, we no longer are limited to a $90,000 mortgage. We can actually now afford a $120,000 mortgage and a house which costs $130,000 or more!

What I've done is not complicated and well worth an additional moment spent in understanding. The emphasis thus far has been on using the GPM to *reduce* the monthly payment. What I am suggesting here is that the other side of the coin works equally well. The GPM can be used to keep a monthly payment (if we know what we can afford) within a budget and increase the mortgage amount and, thereby, the price we can afford to pay.

If we can only afford a $100,000 home under the traditional fixed-rate and ARMs, we probably can afford a $130,000 or bigger home under the GPM. The GPM broadens our horizons considerably.

DISADVANTAGES OF THE GPM

High Monthly Payments Later On

The first big problem with the GPM is the fact that, in order get lower monthly payments during the first 5 or 10 years of the mortgage, we have to accept higher monthly payments for the remainder of the mortgage. If we were to add up the savings we received during the first years of the mortgage and compare them with the amount we paid out during the remainder, we would find they were more than offset.

SAVINGS VERSUS COST OF GPM—$35,000 at 8½ percent for 30 years at 7.5 graduation rate, 5-year graduation term

Year	*Savings per month ($)*	*Annual ($)*
1	66	792
2	51	612
3	24	288
4	17	204
5	−2	−24
6–30	−22	−264 per year

If we add up the total savings for the first four years, they come to $1896.

$ 792	Year one
612	Year two
288	Year three
+ 204	Year four
$1896	Total savings

Then, if we add up the total expenses, we find they come to $6360.

$ 24	Year five
+ 6336	Years six through thirty at $264 per year
$ 6,360	Total expenses

In order to save about $1900 in the first 4 years of the mortgage, we have spent over $6000 during the life of the mortgage. The net cost to us has been $4464.

Looking at it from the long term, it hardly makes sense. However, most of us don't look at it from the long term. The short term is the way we tend to approach these things. How many of us will actually live in the property for 30 years and pay off the mortgage? What about the effects of inflation on our money over 30 years? If we consider the short term, the loss at the end of the mortgage is more than offset by the savings at the beginning.

Problems with Negative Amortization

The second big problem with the GPM is the negative amortization. This comes up very fast. We can find that, within the first few years, our mortgage balance has increased 5 or even 10 percent. This can be a real problem if we have to sell, say for example, after year three. We can find that we have far less equity in the property than we at first thought.

Of course, if we've at the same time seen a big price appreciation, we won't mind. But, if we happened to buy one of those homes in a low-demand area where prices haven't really gone anywhere, by the time we pay sales closing costs and commission, we could find that after 3 years we won't even get our down payment back out of the property. In fact, it's not inconceivable that after 3 years, it might cost us money out of our pocket just to sell the property!

Consider Table 5–1 on page 79 which gave figures for the ARM/GPM. Look at year three. At that time, the mortgage value was $53.408.42. (Original value was $50,000.)

Let's say we had put 10 percent, or $5000, down into the property for a purchase price of $55,000. Now we want to sell.

The property has appreciated only 2 percent a year. It's new value is roughly $58,000.

$55,000	Purchase price
× 6%	Approximate appreciation after 3 years
$3,300	New value

We have a new value of $58,300. When it comes time to sell, we can figure that our costs including commission will be about 10 percent.

$58,300	Property value after 3 years in low-demand area
× 10%	Costs of sale
$ 5,830	Sales costs including commission

Now, we can figure out what we are going to get back into our pocket after 3 years of ownership.

$ 58,300	Sales price
− 5,830	Sales costs
52,470	
− 53,408	Loan balance after 3 years (negative amortization)
− 938	Loss on sale
− 5,000	Down payment
$ − 5,938	Total loss during 3 years of ownership

It's not a pretty picture. In this example, we would have lost nearly $6000 during our 3 years of ownership. It would have probably made more sense to rent.

Of course, the assumption we made was that we purchased in a low-demand area where prices appreciated only 6 percent over 3 years. If price appreciation had been higher, say 5 to 10 percent a year, we would have come out fine. We would have gotten back our original down payment and perhaps even a profit.

The negative amortization feature of the GPM can be a disadvantage. If you get the mortgage, you want to be sure either you're in an area of high demand and rapid appreciation *or* you will be able to keep the house for a long time. Otherwise, be prepared to lose money when it's time to sell.

GPMs are available from a wide variety of lenders, including both banks and savings and loan associations. But, although these institutions may be authorized to offer them, not all do. For many of the more conservative lenders, GPMs are simply too difficult and too risky. Just as in the last example for borrowers, lenders are concerned that they too may end up with a loss. Therefore, you may have to shop around to find them. Federally chartered savings and loans and mortgage bankers are probably your best bet.

SIX

Creative Financing —Nothing Down and a Little a Month

"Creative financing," some knowledgeable people will tell you, is just another word for "seller financing." Instead of going out and having an institutional lender such as a bank or savings and loan association finance the purchase of property, the seller helps the buyer with the financing.

True. But creative financing is also much more than just that. I think that the term "creative" can only be understood in comparison with the term "traditional" financing. Traditional financing is simply this. When a buyer wants, for example, to buy a house, the buyer goes out and secures a new and big first loan from an institutional lender, then the buyer puts the difference between the mortgage and price up in cash. This way if a buyer wants to buy a $100,000 house, he or she would obtain an $80,000 mortgage from a savings and loan association and put up $20,000 in cash.

Note that, in the traditional financing, there is no mention of the seller. The seller does not participate. All of the money borrowing is done by the buyer. As far as the seller is concerned, it's an all-cash sale. The seller receives $100,000 in cash from the buyer. (The buyer on his or her own, of course, has borrowed $80,000 of this amount.)

In creative financing, something else happens. Another way of defining creative financing would be to say that, any time it is less than *all* cash to the seller or more than a single first mortgage to the buyer, it is creative financing. In creative financing, sometimes the seller helps the buyer by giving a mortgage, but other times the seller helps by just arranging an institutional mortgage for a buyer. The best definition of creative financing, therefore, is buyer and seller working together.

THE SECOND MORTGAGE FOR 10 PERCENT

Albert wanted to sell his home for $100,000, and he wanted all cash. Of course, Albert did not own his home free and clear. He actually had a mortgage on it for $18,000. But, he planned to pay off this mortgage with the proceeds from the sale and then keep the rest for himself (after closing costs and commission).

Albert listed his house for sale and waited for a buyer to come along. It took 5 months, but finally one did—Suzy.

Suzy fell in love with Albert's house. She definitely wanted to buy it. She had a good job as an officer in an insurance company and was able to qualify for a new 80 percent adjustable interest-rate mortgage. There was a problem, however. To buy the house, Suzy needed 20 percent, or $20,000, in cash as the down payment. She didn't have it.

The agent who represented Suzy suggested a compromise. "Why not offer the seller $90,000 cash to him and a second mortgage for the remaining $10,000?"

$ 10,000	Suzy's cash
+ 80,000	First mortgage
90,000	Cash to seller
+ 10,000	Second mortgage from seller
$100,000	Price

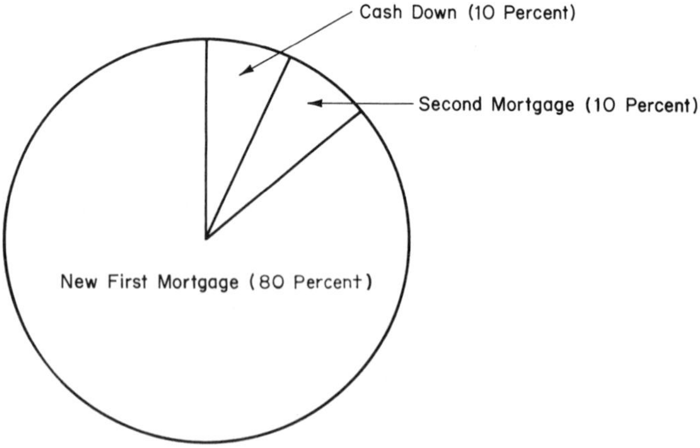

FIGURE 6-1. Suzy's offer.

Suzy saw that she was actually borrowing from the seller the $10,000 that she needed, and in exchange giving him a $10,000 second mortgage (Figure 6-1). She agreed that the second mortgage should bear interest at 15 percent and be payable at $125 per month and that it would be all due and payable in 3 years. (Suzy hoped that within 3 years she would be able to either sell the property or refinance with a new first mortgage for a large enough amount—$90,000—to pay off both her new first and the new second.)

Albert, at first wanted to reject the offer. After all, he wanted all cash to him. This offer was only offering him 90 percent cash. The other 10 percent was paper.

Albert's agent said, "There are several advantages to this offer.

1. "You are getting your price.
2. "Even though $10,000 is in the form of a mortgage and you won't get the cash for 3 years, it will earn interest during that period. After all, if you got the $10,000 in cash, wouldn't you just stick it in the bank and earn interest on it? Here the interest is agreed upon in advance.
3. "You are selling the house."

The agent then noted the one disadvantage. "If you actually need cash, to get it you'll have to sell the mortgage to someone, and that person will normally expect a discount. The discount will be anywhere from 5 to 40 percent. That means if you need cash right away, you'll have to take a loss of from $500 to $4000 on the second. (See Chapter 14.)

Albert didn't have an immediate use for the cash and intended putting it in savings anyhow, so the second made sense for him. He agreed to the sale.

This is probably the most simplified form of creative financing that we are likely to run into. It's not particular to any time or money condition. I was writing these kinds of deals in the 1950s just as agents are writing them today.

In the trade, they are known as 80/10/10s.

80%	First mortgage
10	Second mortgage
+ 10	Cash
100%	

Of course, the buyer might have gotten a 90 percent first mortgage or even a 95 percent. But, the assumption here is that, for one reason or another, the buyer could qualify only for an 80 percent mortgage. Now, let's branch out into a few variations on the kind of deal we've just seen.

THE INSTITUTIONAL SECOND

Let's change the situation a bit. Just prior to the signing of the sales agreement, Albert got an emergency phone call from his brother in Alaska. His brother had the opportunity of a lifetime to bid on some oil drilling contracts. But he needed cash, all the money Albert could raise.

Albert jumped at the chance and told him he would send the money right along. But, that presented a problem. Albert now needed all cash, yet the deal he was being offered was for a second mortgage for $10,000. How could he convert that $10,000 to cash without at the same time having to discount it?

THREE WAYS TO CONVERT A SECOND MORTGAGE TO CASH WITHOUT LOSING THE DISCOUNT

"Since you now need all cash," his broker told him, "there are three ways to handle it, assuming the buyer can't come up with any more cash.

1. "Have the buyer go to a major lender such as a savings and loan association and borrow the $10,000 in a *second* mortgage. Many savings and loans are today giving short-term seconds (due in 3-5 years) in preference to long-term (30 years) fixed-rate firsts. They figure the short due date will help them in a volatile market. We can tell the buyer you want all cash and suggest she go out and borrow it.

"But, there is a problem. In today's market, the S&L will probably want big payments on the second. That means the buyer has to qualify for both a high-interest first *and* a high-interest second, which might be a problem. And there could still be a small discount of 4 or 5 percent.

2. "Or you could go directly to a mortgage broker (not banker) and borrow the money on a second mortgage yourself. In some cases, these mortgages are then *assumable*. You borrow the $10,000 and then the buyer *assumes* your second mortgage.

"Of course, there's the discount. In the first two ways, someone is going to have to pay a discount—usually between 4 and 12 percent. You'll get your money out this way, but you might still have to take a little bit less.

3. "There's a final way to handle this. We could jack up the price of your home a little bit, say $2000. That way, instead of getting a $10,000 second, your second mortgage would be for $12,000. Now, when you go to discount it by 20 percent, you'll be getting all your cash out ($10,000) even after the discount."

Financing the Discount

"But," Albert looked troubled, "is that fair?"

"Yes," the broker said, "if both you and the seller agree and the person you sold your second to (as well as the lender of the first) are aware of the circumstances. What we're doing here is moving the discount onto the back of the buyer. But, to make it an easy burden, it's in the form of additional amounts on the second mortgage. It's all paper not due for another 3 years."

"I still don't get it," Albert said. "Why does increasing the price move the burden to the buyer?"

"Quite simply," the broker explained further, "we can break it down into three distinct actions:

1. "The buyer is paying more for the property, in this case $2000 more.

2. "That $2000 is not coming from the buyer in cash nor from an additional amount of the first mortgage, but is coming in the form of an increase in the second (from $10,000 to $12,000).

3. "That increase in the second corresponds to the discount that you'll have to pay to cash out the second, so you get your money in cash."

Albert nodded.

"By paying $2000 more for the house, the buyer is paying the cost of the discount. The buyer probably won't object, however, because that $2000 is not in the form of cash from the buyer, but in the form of a second mortgage."

Finally Albert understood.

The second mortgage is a basic device used in arranging creative financing, and we'll have more to say about it in a later chapter.

But, for now, let's consider a different set of circumstances.

USING SECONDARY FINANCING TO REDUCE THE DOWN AND TO LOWER MONTHLY PAYMENTS

Shirley had a house she wanted to sell, and the price she was asking was $100,000. But, Shirley's house backed right up to a fire station. Whenever there was a fire, the trucks roared out, sirens blazing. In addition to all the problems she had in selling her home in a tight market, she also had to contend with the poor location of her property.

Shirley, of course, wanted to sell for all cash. But, it quickly became apparent that no cash buyer was going to make an offer unless she lowered her price significantly, which she refused to do. So, to get her price, she was going to have to make her property somehow more appealing. How?

By offering creative financing.

Shirley has an existing first mortgage on her property for $40,000. Her mortgage is with a state-chartered savings and loan association, and one of the clauses in the mortgage specifically states that, on the sale of the property, the mortgage is due and payable (a due-on clause).

But, Shirley's broker told her that in the state she was living, at the present time, the courts ruled that the due-on clause was unenforceable. If she was willing to take a chance that the legislature or the courts wouldn't change the law retroactively (a tiny possibility), she could force the lender on the first mortgage to allow a new buyer to assume it.

Advantage of an Assumable First

Shirley's agent, Carl, pointed out that there was a big advantage to having an assumable first. "Your first mortgage is for 10 percent interest. That's a big incentive to a buyer in today's market where interest rates are much, much higher."

"But,"Shirley lamented, "my first is only for $40,000. I want $100,000 for my property. Where is the buyer going to get the other $60,000?"

"You're going to have to help the buyer out. You're going to have to give the buyer financing. But, it won't be so bad. You're going to get a good rate of interest on whatever mortgage you take back."

Shirley listed her house, agreeing to help with the financing. It was on the market for over 3 months without a single nibble. Carl pointed out that being near the fire station was a real drawback.

Finally, another agent brought in a potential buyer, Dorothy. Dorothy really didn't mind the fire station and she liked Shirley's house. She wanted to buy.

However, Dorothy had some real problems.

1. She had been divorced and had two small children she was raising. Her alimony, child support, and money from a job she held only allowed her to make payments of a maximum of $800 a month, not including taxes and insurance (which she could pay extra).

2. She only had $5000 cash to put down. However, her rich uncle had died and she expected an inheritance which she would receive within 6 months.

"Only $5000 down and with payments not more than $800 a month," Shirley wailed. "She can't possible afford to buy my property." Shirley was convinced there could be no deal.

But, Carl indicated that there might indeed be a way. "It all depends on how 'motivated' you are to sell," he said. "If you really want to get out and are willing to accept a higher risk, then we may very well be able to sell to Dorothy using creative financing."

Shirley said she did indeed want to sell and was listening closely.

Carl said that Dorothy, the buyer, had two problems—she was low on cash for an initial period of 6 months, and she couldn't afford high monthly payments. Carl asked how much the payments on the existing first mortgage (which was assumable) were.

Shirley said they were $400 a month.

"That means," Carl continued, "that Dorothy can't pay more than $400 monthly more on secondary financing. But, that should be enough. I think we can work out a deal."

Here's the deal that Carl proposed (Figure 6–2).

$ 5,000	Down payment in cash
40,000	Existing first mortgage to be assumed by Dorothy
40,000	New second mortgage to be given by Shirley to Dorothy
11,000	New *third* mortgage to be given by Shirley to Dorothy
+ 4,000	New *fourth* mortgage to be given by Shirley to Carl!
$100,000	Full purchase price

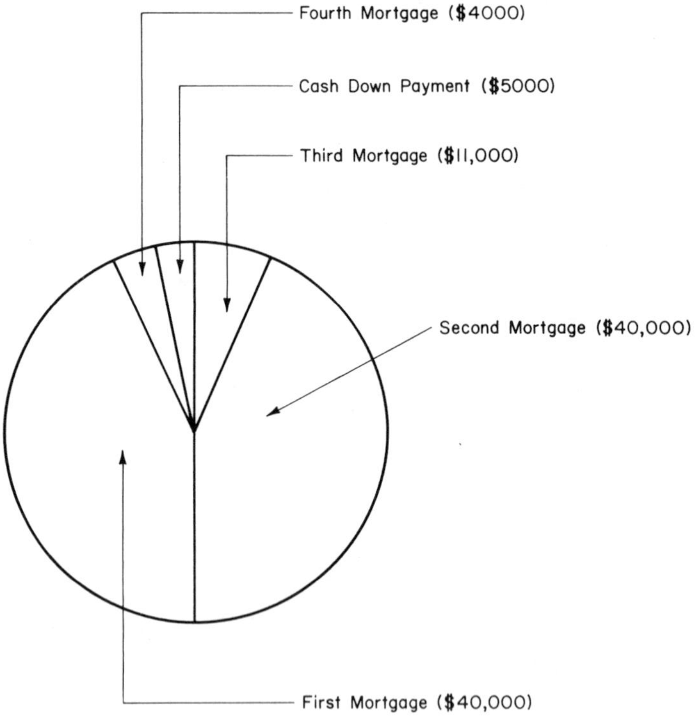

FIGURE 6-2. Carl's proposal.

Shirley looked at the figures and shook her head, "I don't understand this. The way you have it, I'm giving Dorothy two mortgages, a second and a third, and you're giving her a fourth. It doesn't make sense."

"It makes perfect sense,"Carl said. "I'll take it one step at a time so you can see how it works:"

Taking It One Step at a Time

1. "A $5000 down payment. This is easy and straightforward. Dorothy gives you $5000 down.

2. "A $40,000 first mortgage. Again, this is straightforward. This is your current first mortgage from XYZ Savings and Loan. Because of the state laws prohibiting S&Ls from exercising their due-on clause, XYZ may allow Dorothy to assume this mortgage at the old 10 percent interest rate.

3. "A $40,000 second mortgage. Again, this is not complicated. This is the second mortgage or the loan you are giving Dorothy to help her buy the property. We'll make it all due and payable to you in 5 years. In the meantime, you'll collect interest at 16 percent a year."

"Sixteen percent," Shirley sucked in her breath. "How much interest will that be?"

"It's easy to figure.

$40,000	Second mortgage
× 16%	Interest rate
6,400	Annual interest
÷ 12	Months/year
$ 533	Monthly interest

"You'll be getting $6400 a year."

"I see a problem," Shirley observed. "To pay just the interest on my mortgage, it will cost $533 a month. And to pay the interest on the first mortgage, it will cost $400 a month.

$ 400	Payment on first mortgage
+ 533	Payment on second mortgage
$ 933	Total payment

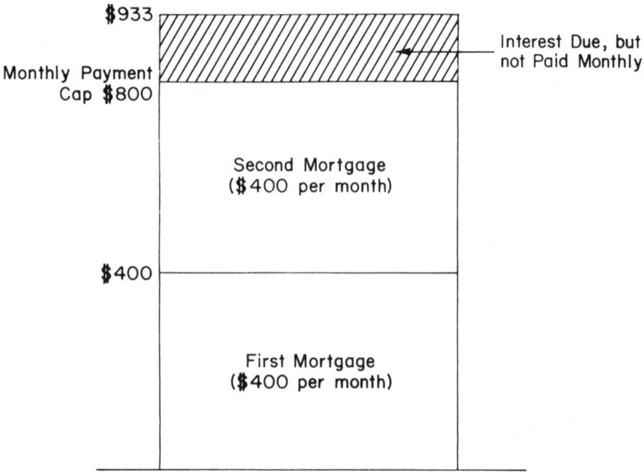

FIGURE 6-3. Capping the monthly payment.

"That means that Dorothy will need to come up with $933 a month just for the first and second. But, we already know she can't pay more than $800 a month in total payments. Where is she going to get the additional $133?"

"She's going to borrow it from you," Carl answered.

Shirley looked puzzled.

"It's simple. We just write the second so that the monthly payments are $400 a month, and $400 on the first and $400 on the second add up to exactly $800."

"That's just what Dorothy can afford."

"But, if we do that, then I won't get my full interest."

"Yes you will. We'll add the additional interest on to the second mortgage. Each month Dorothy will owe you $133 more, plus interest. It's called "negative amortization." (See the discussion in the previous chapter.)

Shirley nodded. "I, in effect, loan her the money to make the payments by adding it to the amount of the second mortgage."

"Precisely."

4. "Finally, there's the matter of the third mortgage."

"Yes," Shirley interrupted. "I really don't have any idea of what you're talking about there."

When the Seller Gives the Buyer Two Mortgages on the Same House

"There can be as many mortgages as anyone is willing to lend money on property," Carl explained. "There can be first through tenth or twentieth or five hundreth. What's critical is that there be sufficient equity in the property to act as collateral for the mortgage. In the event that a borrower defaults, the first mortgage is entitled to first money. The second to second money, the third to third money and so on. If the house is worth $100,000 and the first is $40,000, that lender in a foreclosure takes all his or her money ($40,000) out first."

"If the second is for $40,000, that lender takes all his or her money out next. If the third is for $11,000, that lender has to take what's left. If there's $9000 left, that lender gets paid some. If not, that lender and all succeeding lenders lose." (See the next chapter for a further discussion.)

"What I'm getting at is that there's nothing strange or unusual about having a third mortgage on a house."

"Yes," Shirley countered, "but how can I have *both* a second and a third?"

"You can have as many as you want. You could have a first, second, third, fourth, and fifth, if you and a buyer/borrower agreed."

Shirley nodded, "But, what about your fourth?"

Giving the Broker a Mortgage for the Commission

"Aha," Carl smiled. "There's the matter of my commission. I'm charging you 6 percent, or $6000, to sell your home. In addition, you have closing costs to pay which will cost you about $3000. That comes to $9000. Where are you going to get the money to pay me if you are only getting $5000 in a down payment?

$ 9,000	Closing costs and commission
− 5,000	Down payment
$− 4,000	Cash needed to close deal

"Do you have $4000 you can let me have?"

Shirley shook her head. All her money was tied up in the property. "Besides," she replied angrily, "even if I had the money, I wouldn't want to spend it. I expect to get money out of the sale, not put it in!"

Carl nodded, "Of course. That's why we have a fourth mortgage. You'll recall that Dorothy said she expects to get a big inheritance in 6 months. I propose we make both the third and fourth mortgages due in 6 months. They will all come due and payable then. I will hold off on the payment of my $4000 commission until then, and when Dorothy pays, I'll get paid and so will you."

Shirley nodded. That kind of made sense. "Only," she added, "how can Dorothy make payments on the third and fourth mortgages? She's already up to her maximum of $800 monthly with the first and second."

Arranging It So the Buyer Has no Monthly Payments on the Mortgages

"What payments on the third and fourth?" Carl asked. There are no payments on it. It's all due and payable in 6 months, including interest at 16 percent a year.

$11,000	$11,000	Third mortgage amount
× 16%		Interest rate *per year*
$ 1,760		
	+ 880	*6 months* interest
	$11,880	Due from Dorothy in 6 months

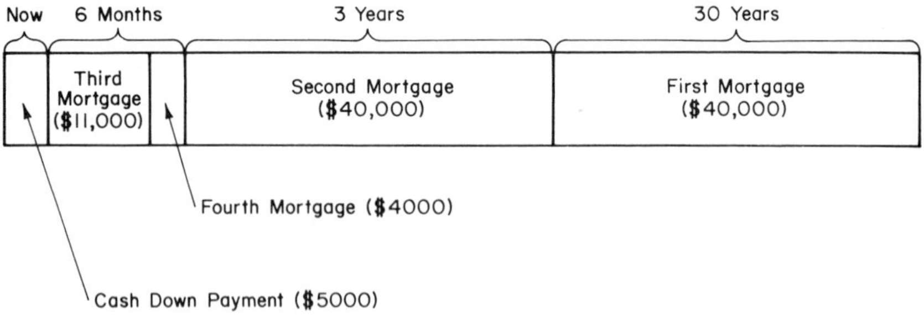

FIGURE 6-4. Cash flow over 30 years with low down payment.

"At the end of 6 months, she'll pay you $11,000 plus interest. The same will happen to me and my fourth. You'll have sold your property, have cash back, plus a big second mortgage. And don't forget the extra interest you're making on the third."

Shirley nodded. It seemed better all the time. "There's just one thing. Why would Dorothy go for this deal? She's paying all kinds of interest everywhere."

"She'll go for it," Carl explained, "because it's a good deal for her. She's buying a house she likes for only $5000 down and only $800 a month (not counting taxes and insurance). Where else is she going to find a deal like that?

"Of course, there's the third she'll have to pay off plus interest. But, she's expecting the money in 6 months so that's no big deal. And, if she had borrowed $15,000 to close the deal from a bank, you can be sure she would pay a lot more than 16 percent interest.

"As far as the second mortgage is concerned, I'm sure she's confident that within 3 years she can refinance the house or sell to get out from under it. For Dorothy, it's as good a deal as it is for you."

THE DRAWBACK TO THE "GOOD DEAL"

In the past few years, I've seen many such deals made. They are, in fact, "good deals," *if* everything works out as planned. If it doesn't, however, they can be very bad deals. My concern is that, too often, the potential disadvantages (problems that may indeed never happen) never get pointed out. Here are some of the problems with Shirley's, Carl's, and Dorothy's deal that I see.

Possible Problems for the Buyer

From Dorothy's, the buyer's, viewpoint, the biggest single danger lies in the short-term third mortgage. True, she is expecting money in from an inheritance to pay off that mortgage. But, what if there's a delay? What if the inheritance is smaller than expected? What if the inheritance taxes are larger? What if there is a legal challenge by another relative?

The "what ifs" could go on indefinitely and not one of us would live our lives if we spent all out time worrying about "what ifs." But, there's an important point to consider. It's one thing to have money in your hand, quite another to have it owed to you. Money in your hand you can spend confidently. Money owed to you can only be spent with trepidation. Dorothy ended up spending money owed to her. If it gets paid to her, she can pay Shirley and Carl. If not . . .?

If not, Shirley and Carl would be within their rights to immediately begin foreclosure proceedings on the property and take it back from Dorothy. Dorothy would lose her new house and her down payment. (Of course, it could be argued that it won't be such a great loss since Dorothy only put up $5000.)

Possible Problems for the Seller

From Shirley's, the seller's, viewpoint, the danger lies in the small down payment that Dorothy put up. If Dorothy doesn't pay on the third or the second, or the first mortgages, Shirley must foreclose to protect her interest in the property. Shirley is gambling that Dorothy will pay.

She may have Dorothy's good intentions and her integrity to count on here. But, with only $5000 down, she has very little of Dorothy's money. If the inheritance doesn't work out or if Dorothy loses her job, or her alimony or child support doesn't come in, Dorothy might just walk away.

If Dorothy walks away, that might just be the beginning of the problems for Shirley. Shirley would have to begin foreclosure proceedings. That could be costly. With lost interest payments and foreclosure costs, it could be anywhere from $2000 to $6000 or $7000. We'll say it's $5000. It could cost Shirley $5000 to foreclose and take back the house.

Of course, it might be argued that she received $5000 in down payment and so she broke even.

Wrong. Remember, there were closing costs she had to pay on the sale *including* Carl's commission!

−$ 3,000	Closing costs of sale
− 2,000	Carl's commission (not including fourth)
− 5,000	Foreclosure costs including interest payments on all mortgages
−10,000	Total costs to Shirley
+ 5,000	Down payment originally given by Dorothy
−$ 5,000	Loss on attempted sale

Shirley might indeed end up with the property back, but, it also might cost her $5000 in personal expenses.

THE DOWN PAYMENT IS CRUCIAL

The big point to understand here is the value of the down payment.

Institutional lenders such as savings and loan associations, banks, and others will not normally lend more than 80 percent of the purchase price of a home without some form of mortgage insurance on the amount over 80 percent. (See the discussion on mortgage insurance in Chapter 7.)

The reason is the very problem that Shirley might run up against. If they do have to foreclose, that margin, that 20 percent, acts as a cushion to absorb expenses so that they don't incur any loss.

Shirley, however, because she was desperate to sell, did not maintain an adequate margin. She settled for too low a down payment to ensure her equity in the property. If Dorothy does not make her payments, Shirley loses.

How Big a Down Payment Is Minimum?

The answer to that is simple. It's an amount sufficient to cover:

1. All closing costs including commission
2. Any costs of potential foreclosure
3. Any costs of refurbishing the house and putting it on the market again
4. Any costs of effort and time on the part of Shirley in handling a possible foreclosure

That's the minimum amount. In actual dollars, it depends on the terms of each deal, but generally speaking, it is *never* less than 10 percent and is usually between 15 and 20 percent of the purchase price. Any seller accepting less is taking an additional risk.

I'm not saying that Shirley shouldn't have accepted the deal that Carl put together and that Dorothy offered. I'm merely pointing out the potential problems that lie within it. You, the reader, should similarly beware of deals in which you sell property for a small down payment. Sometimes they work out beautifully. And sometimes they don't. I personally have been involved in situations both ways and I can assure you that if you should have to foreclose on a deal in which you didn't accept enough of a down payment, you very quickly stop patting yourself on the back for your acumen in originally selling your property.

In today's tight market, I think it's a situation in which sellers who are desperate to sell take any kind of offer. But, it could be a matter of jumping out of the frying pan into the fire.

Finally, from Carl's viewpoint, this was also no terrific deal. Carl did all the work of an agent including bringing buyer and seller together. However, upon sale, Carl received only $2000 in cash. The rest he had to take in a fourth. His risk is similar to Shirley's. If Dorothy goes into default and doesn't pay on the fourth, he's not going to get his money unless he tries to foreclose. This might involve first paying off Dorothy! It's a lot of effort for Carl on a not very sure thing.

An extreme form of the above transaction has been occurring in many areas of the country involving no money down or even money back to the *buyer* upon purchase. These transactions are great, when they work. But, too often, they involve a problem that Shirley ran into—little or no money down from the buyer and a foreclosure. If that happens, then the seller is usually in trouble and stands to lose money.

NO MONEY DOWN

In this type of transaction, the situation could be very similar to that between Shirley and Dorothy. The difference would be that, instead of Dorothy putting $5000 down, she would put nothing down. Instead, she might give Shirley a fifth mortgage for the down payment (or perhaps a promissory note).

$ 5,000	Fifth mortgage
4,000	Fourth mortgage
11,000	Third mortgage
40,000	Second mortgage
+ 40,000	Existing first assumed
$100,000	Purchase price

As can be seen, the deal works out in terms of the numbers. However, from a practical viewpoint, the monthly payments and

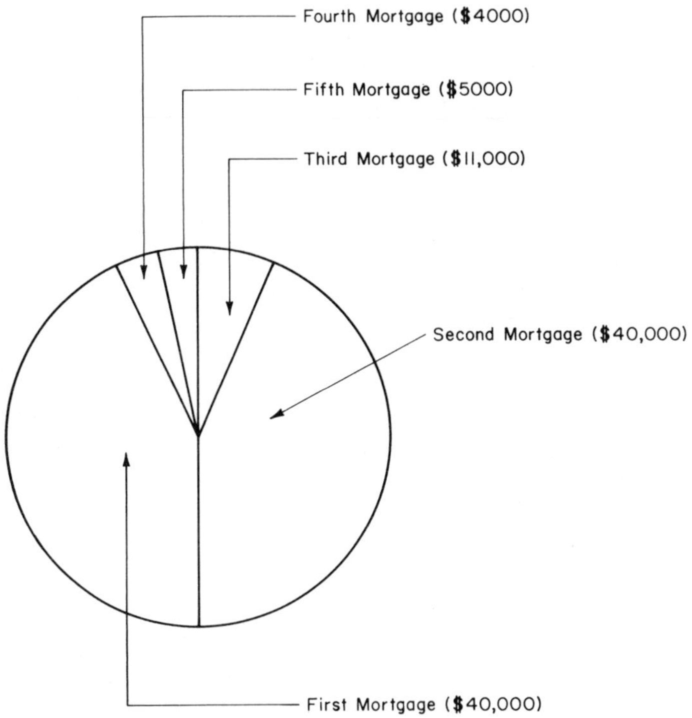

FIGURE 6–5. No-money-down financing.

payback might be a problem. In such deals, I've seen the payback schedule look something like this:

$ 5,000	Fifth, due in 1 year, no interest
4,000	Fourth, due in 1 year, no interest
11,000	Third, due in 2 years, 16% interest, no monthly payments
40,000	Second, due in 5 years, 16% interest, payable monthly at less than enough to pay interest, so negative amortization occurs
+ 40,000	First assumed by buyer
$100,000	

The seller in this situation has *no cash* from the buyer. Usually, the broker is willing to take a commission sometime in the future. To

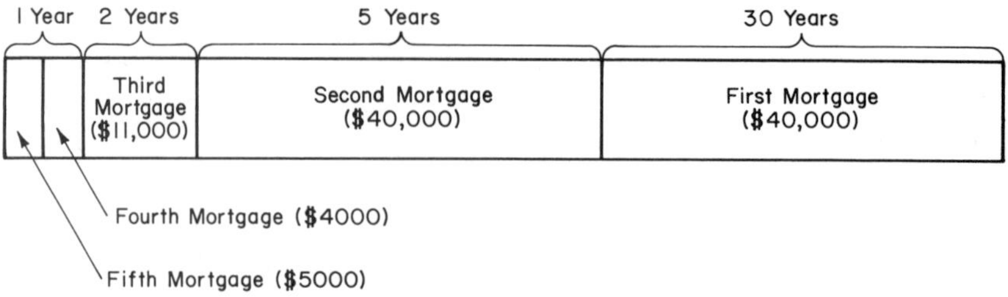

FIGURE 6–6. Cash flow over 30 years with no down payment.

make the sale, the seller may have to actually take money out of his or her pocket to pay for closing costs.

The danger, of course, is that, for the seller, if the buyer doesn't make the payments, a foreclosure would mean more money spent (plus the cost of the commission).

In this no-money-down deal, there is increased danger from the fact that there are no payments due on the fifth or the fourth and less than the actual amount of interest is paid on the second. This means that the buyer/borrower could actually be in trouble and have no chance of paying back the third or the fourth. But, because there are no monthly payments due, the seller might not know about it until these higher mortgages come due, a year later. Since foreclosure can take anywhere from several months to years, there could be additional costs in lost interest.

From the buyer's viewpoint, this is a house built of cards. The buyer in such circumstances usually assumes that the value of the property will go up sufficiently so that by the end of a year, he or she can refinance and get enough money to pay off the fourth and fifth.

If this doesn't happen, the buyer usually just walks away from the deal. After all, the only thing the buyer has invested is the monthly payments, and if the house was rented out for the monthly payment, the buyer doesn't even have his or her own money in it at all.

Perhaps the wildest form of this is when the buyer actually gets cash back upon purchase. I've seen this done in at least two ways.

MONEY BACK TO BUYER ON PURCHASE

New Homes

In one instance, builders of new homes have been offering cash bonuses back to buyer upon the purchase of one of their homes. The homes may be selling for $200,000. The buyer puts 10 percent, or $20,000, down. The seller/contractor arranges for a lender to come up with 90 percent, or $180,000, in a first mortgage. The buyer has only one mortgage for $180,000.

However, after the deal closes, as a bonus for buying, the contractor refunds or rebates to the buyer $25,000 to be used as the buyer wishes!

Consider this deal. The buyer puts up $20,000 and buys a home with a single first mortgage at competitive rates. Then the buyer gets $25,000 back. Even after closing costs, this buyer has really made out.

The key, of course, is the monthly payments. The buyer is stuck with a mortgage at perhaps 15 percent interest. A 15 percent interest mortgage amortized for 30 years means monthly payments of about $2400. That's a terrific burden. It means that to qualify, a buyer should be making roughly four times the monthly payment, or $10,000 a month or $120,000 per year! There just aren't too many buyers in that category. What too often happens is that buyers far less able to make the monthly payments cheat on their loan application statements, buy the property, and then use the $25,000 rebate to help make their payments. They sometimes figure that if they take that $25,000 and use $1000 of it each month to offset their $2400 payment, it comes down to $1400. They can go on that way for more than 2 years before they run out of supplemental money and then they can sell for a profit, they hope.

Maybe they can and maybe they can't. A lot depends on the market conditions at the time they decide to bail out. If they happen to end up in a very tight market, they could lose everything.

The second instance I have seen is far more complicated and, in my estimation, far more incredible.

RESALE CASH BACK TO BUYER

Let's go back to Shirley and say that the deal she was going to make with Dorothy didn't work out. The very next day, another broker brought her a different deal. It looked like this:

$ 80,000	New first mortgage
40,000	New second mortgage to Shirley
+ 20,000	Cash to Shirley
$140,000	Purchase price

Shirley at first couldn't understand what was happening. The buyer was offering her $40,000 *more* than she was asking.

Carl explained it to her. "The buyer is going to get a *new* first mortgage for $80,000. Then he's going to give *you* a $40,000 second as before and $20,000 cash."

Shirley couldn't understand why the price was $140,000 when she received the same amount of money as before, $100,000.

"It's really simple," Carl said. "This buyer is going to share the proceeds of the new $80,000 first mortgage with you."

$ 80,000	New first
− 40,000	First to be paid off
40,000	Cash
− 20,000	To Shirley
$ 20,000	To new buyer

"Do you mean to tell me that the new buyer is actually going to get money back out of this deal?"

"That's correct," Carl said. "The buyer will put nothing into the property, but upon closing the deal, will get $20,000 in cash out."

Of course, the danger in this transaction is all to Shirley. It comes in the form of her $40,000 second mortgage. You'll recall that before, her second mortgage had as collateral her equity in the property. The house was worth $100,000, there was a $40,000 first, and the second could claim the next $40,000 of equity. She had a margin of $20,000 between her mortgage and the house's value.

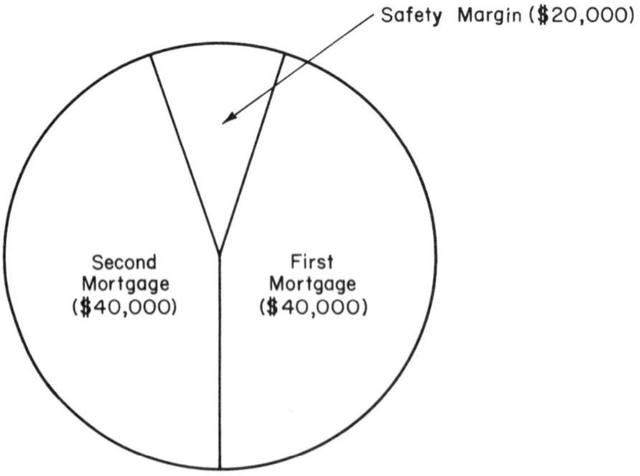

FIGURE 6–7. Traditional creative financing.

Old deal

$ 40,000	First mortgage
+ 40,000	Second mortgage
80,000	Total mortgages
+ 20,000	Margin
$100,000	House value

New Deal

$ 80,000	First mortgage
+ 40,000	Second mortgage
120,000	Total mortgages
100,000	House value
– $ 20,000	Margin

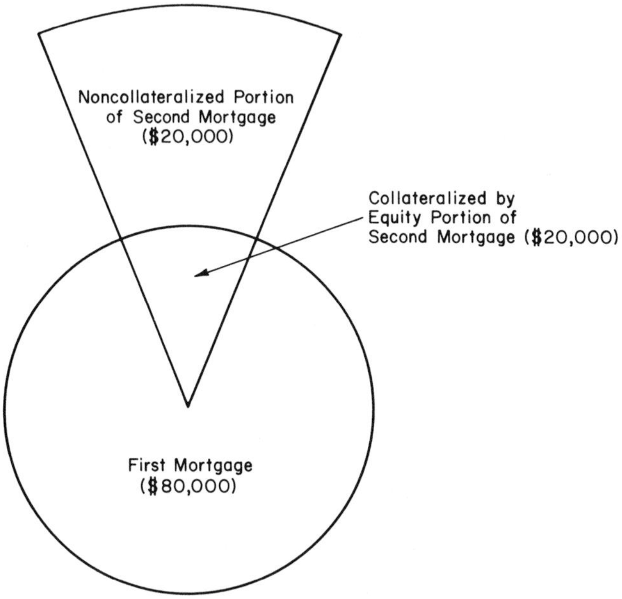

FIGURE 6–8. Money back to buyer/equity loss for seller.

In this new deal, Shirley would have a negative margin. That is to say her second mortgage for $40,000 would be for $20,000 *more* than the house was actually worth! (Remember, the house didn't change value in the second deal. Regardless of the price, it still is only worth $100,000.)

The Danger to the Seller in Cash Back to Buyer

Shirley's danger here would be both real and immediate. If the buyer didn't keep up the payments and Shirley had to foreclose, not only would she be out the closing costs and possibly the commission on the sale, but she'd also stand an excellent chance of losing the $20,000 in cash the buyer got.

Her potential loss if the buyer didn't keep up the payments could amount to as much as:

– $ 3,000	Original closing costs
– 6,000	Commission
– 5,000	Costs of foreclosure including lost interest
– 20,000	Loss on second mortgage because house couldn't be sold for enough to pay it off
– $34,000	Total loss to Shirley

To sell this, *if* things don't go right for Shirley, could cost her $35,000 or more than half of her equity in the property. The downside risk here in almost every similar case I've seen far outweighs any advantage that may come from a quick sale.

From the buyer's viewpoint, I don't see how we could get a better deal. No money down, cash back on purchase, and a fairly long term (3 to 5 years) on the second.

Most buyers using this technique that I've seen have no intention of living in the property themselves. They usually intend to just rent it out and then use the monthly rental, supplemented in part by the cash back on purchase, to make their payments on the first and second mortgages. They hope that in time they'll be able to sell for enough of a profit to pay off both mortgages and leave some money left over for them.

Of course, if things don't work out, they usually feel they can walk away and the sooner the better. After all, this buyer gets his or her profit before resale! He or she gets it the day of purchase!

CRANKABLES

There's another variety of this technique which investors have been using of late. It involves finding a piece of property, usually a house or other residential building (two or four units) which are termed "crankable." The way it works is described below.

Cranking Out Cash Through a Refinance

Susan is a real estate investor. She's looking for a particular piece of property. She finds it in the form of a house owned by Emerson.

Emerson has been transferred out of the state. He must sell and sell immediately. Yet, in his area, the market is very weak and, try as he might, he can't find any buyers. After going with several agents, Emerson has lowered his price and is now trying to sell "by owner." His price is $100,000.

Susan finds Emerson's house and makes him this deal:

$ 50,000	Existing first bought "subject to"
+ 50,000	Second "subordinated"
$100,000	Purchase price

Susan is offering Emerson the full price for his property. But, she's added two new terms to the mortgages which we haven't dealt with yet. Let's consider them:

Subject to: This simply means that Susan will not assume the obligation to pay back the first mortgage. The obligation will lie with Emerson and with the house as collateral.

Subordinated: This is a very important term. When installed in a second or other junior mortgage, it means that mortgage will always remain junior or subordinate to a higher mortgage.

This really isn't very complicated. Let's say we have both a first and a second mortgage on the property. What makes the first a first and the second a second? The answer is the time at which they were recorded. The first mortgage was first because it was recorded first in time. The second was second because it was recorded after the first.

Now, let's say that the borrower fully pays off the first mortgage. It's removed from the property. Where there had been two mortgages, there now is only one. Is that one a first or a second?

Normally, the old second advances and now becomes a first. *Unless* it has been subordinated. In that case, the second would remain a second for the life of the mortgage. It would remain a second *even if there were no first before it!*

Why would Susan insist on the first being "subject to" and the second being "subordinated"?

Just in case the lender on the first mortgage had a due-on clause that was enforceable, Susan might be planning not to mention anything about the sale to the lender! With a due-on clause that was enforceable, if Susan attempted to assume the mortgage after a sale, it would immediately come due and payable. With a subject-to purchase, the lender might never know that the original borrower had sold the property to a new house buyer (until the transfer was recorded).

Finally, and most important, if Susan decided to "walk away" from the property, she wouldn't be liable for payment. She never *borrowed* the money. A foreclosure would not show up against her name on the first.

With regard to the second, Susan might want a subordination clause because this would make the property "crankable."

Consider, with a subordinated second, once the purchase has been made, Susan has the option of going out and getting a new first mortgage—*without paying off the existing second!*

On this property, the second, is for $50,000 and the first is for $50,000. After the purchase is consummated, Susan immediately goes out and refinances. She obtains a new first mortgage for 80 percent of the property value, or $80,000 without touching the second.

Mortgages at time of purchase

$ 50,000	First
+ 50,000	Second
$100,000	Purchase price

Mortgages after 1 month (refinanced)

$ 80,000	First
+ 50,000	Second
$130,000	Total mortgage value

By keeping the existing second mortgage in place and putting in a new higher first mortgage, Susan has generated $30,000 in cash for herself.

$ 80,000	New first
– 50,000	Existing first paid off
$ 30,000	Cash to Susan

In the terminology of the trade, Susan has "cranked" $30,000 out of the property.

But where has that $30,000 come from? Has it come out of thin air? Remember, we said the property was worth $100,000. But, now it has mortgages on it for $130,000. Did the property suddenly increase in value by $30,000?

Hardly. The cash Susan generated was directly offset by a loss in the equity protecting Emerson's second.

When property sold

$100,000	Value
– 50,000	Existing first
$ 50,000	Equity protecting Emerson's $50,000 second

When property refinanced

$100,000	Value
– 80,000	New first
$ 20,000	Equity protecting Emerson's $50,000 second

Susan has turned Emerson's collateral into cash for herself. She has cranked the property. She put nothing down and received $30,000 in cash on the refinance.

Other Crankables

Investor's are always looking for crankables. They don't always have to take the form shown here. On some occasions, the investor (Susan) might leave the first and give the seller a third mortgage on the property. In recent times, with interest rates being so high, many sellers have been willing to lend money on thirds to get a sale without seriously considering whether or not there was sufficient collateral to warrant the mortgage. In such a case, the deal might look like this:

$ 50,000	Existing first
30,000	New second from outside investor
+ 50,000	*New* third from seller
130,000	Total mortgages on property
− 100,000	Property value
$ 30,000	Mortgages over property value

Our outside investor (usually a mortgage broker) here put up $30,000. Our seller put up $50,000 for essentially very little collateral. And that leads to the practice which has become common for investors such as Susan in today's market.

Crankables worked out fine for virtually everyone when real estate prices were shooting upward almost daily. But, once prices stabilized during the high–interest-rate period of the last year or two, the crankables didn't work. Consider it from Susan's viewpoint.

Problems with Crankables

Why should Susan continue making payments on a first and a second and even a third, when she has no cash invested in the property and when the property is mortgaged for $30,000 more than its value?

There might be a moral reason, but there certainly can be no economic one, once it becomes apparent that the property isn't going to appreciate in value. So Susan and thousands of investors like her in a tight money market simply walk away from the property. She is saying in effect, "I'm not going to pay anymore. Sue me if you can catch me."

Now, consider the plight of Emerson with his big third of $50,000 with only $20,000 collateral behind it. What is he to do?

He can foreclose. In Emerson's case, he would take the property back and find most of his $50,000 was gone. He only had $20,000 in equity. He would find that the foreclosure costs would be more than the equity in the property! It would cost him more to foreclose than he could recoup. He'd be better off just forgetting the whole thing.

Except for one last hope for both of these—the "deficiency judgment."

Deficiency Judgment

If either Emerson or the new investor decide to foreclose through court action (something which is not required in more than half the states), then the court will sell the property at auction to satisfy the mortgages against it.

If the property does not bring sufficient money to pay off all the mortgages, the borrower could be held personally liable for the deficiency. The court could order a "deficiency judgment," and once ordered, Emerson or the innocent investor could attempt to attach bank accounts and other property of Susan to recoup the money lost.

Deficiency judgments are seldom seen during times of rapid price appreciation. During periods of stability or price decline, however, they are common. We are seeing many more deficiency judgments today than at any time during the past 40 years.

Of course, a deficiency judgment is not a panacea. To execute it, Emerson must find Susan, must find assets, and must tie them up. Along with the foreclosure process (which could take up to 2 or 3 years) the whole procedure could be very lengthy—and costly. And for Emerson there could be another drawback, a "purchase-money law."

(A little-used section of the bankruptcy law could allow the borrower to prevent foreclosure for 2 or 3 years and, if and when it came, prevent a deficiency judgment. Have your attorney check the bankruptcy laws if you're in that situation.

Purchase-Money Mortgages

A good many states have purchase-money laws. Put most simply, these state that if a mortgage is given as part of the purchase price on a house (and sometimes other property), no deficiency judgment is allowed in the event the property sells for less than the mortgage value at a foreclosure sale.

Emerson gave Susan the $50,000 second as part of the sales price at the time of the sale. Therefore, in a state which had a purchase money law, he probably could never secure a deficiency judgment.

Our innocent investor, however, because his was a "hard-money loan," or one that was cash advanced and not equity, might very well secure a deficiency judgment. His might not be a purchase-money mortgage.

Crankables are but one more aspect of the no-money-down, cash-back-to-buyer technique used by many buyers and investors of real estate. When they work out and everyone prospers, no one can knock them. But, in hard times, there's the piper to pay and, too often in such cases, these techniques backfire on all concerned. But usually the seller is hardest hit.

Once we have the concept of crankables and no money down (money back on purchase), the variations on the theme are almost endless and are limited only by the imagination of the investor.

Paper Down

One variation which I have seen used with increasing frequency is the paper down. It has an interesting genesis.

Alger wanted to sell his property and Darlene wanted to buy. But, Darlene had her own house to sell before she could buy Alger's. The trouble was that Darlene had no buyers. So she came up with an interesting idea. Instead of giving Alger cash down for his property, she would give him a second mortgage on her old house. Alger's property was $100,000; Darlene's was $80,000.

Alger's Sale

$ 40,000	Second mortgage on Darlene's old house
+ 60,000	Existing first mortgage assumed by Darlene
$100,000	Purchase price

Alger got his price and Darlene got her new house.

Of course, there's the matter of her old home.

Darlene's old home

$ 40,000	Second in favor of Alger
+ 40,000	Existing first
$ 80,000	Value of property

Darlene had mortgaged her old house to the hilt and, in order to make the payments on the first and the second, she's taken it off the market and is renting it out. Because Darlene is a determined and honest person, she intends making all her payments and, eventually, when the market gets better, selling her old home and paying off Alger.

Many deals have been made in this fashion with no ill consequences. However, some enterprising investors took a look at the structure of the deal and saw that it could be adapted to something a bit less desirable.

We'll say that, at the last minute, Darlene pulled out of the deal and Alger was left still trying to sell his house. At this point, Dorene, an investor, came across it.

Dorene had just purchased a home on the following terms:

$ 40,000	Second
+ 40,000	First
$ 80,000	Value and total mortgages

She had bought for nothing down and she had the home mortgaged up to the full value. Now she was ready to do something with the property. She might have tried to trade it to Alger, except that he wanted to sell, not get another piece of property.

So Dorene offered Alger a $40,000 third on her property.

Dorene's offer

$ 40,000	First
40,000	Second
+ 40,000	Third
120,000	Mortgages
− 80,000	Property value
$ 40,000	Over mortgages

Dorene was essentially offering Alger nothing. But he was desperate to sell and he really didn't know property values. He only saw that she was giving him a legitimate third mortgage for $40,000 (legitimate in that the papers were all correctly drawn). He agreed to sell.

Of course, the results should be obvious. Dorene got Alger's house and $40,000 in equity in it for nothing. Alger got a worthless piece of paper on which Dorene stopped making payments. It's an old story and it's just told here as a word to the wise about what to avoid.

What we've discussed so far in creative financing has primarily involved secondary financing—second mortgages, third mortgages, and so forth.

There are other techniques, however, which are used and which do not involve this secondary financing at all. One that is gaining a lot of attention is the "Rich Uncle" technique.

RICH UNCLE TECHNIQUE

The genesis of this idea goes back to the concept of wealthy family members helping poorer family members buy homes. The poor family member bought the house, the "rich uncle" put up the down payment. Ultimately when the house was sold, the rich uncle got his money back plus interest. The poor family member got back any appreciation.

In the modern verson there are usually two unrelated people. One is the home buyer (sometimes an investor, sometimes a person who actually intends to live in the property). The other is the "uncle," always another investor who has a lot of money to invest.

The home buyer usually qualifies for whatever financing happens to be available. The uncle puts up the down payment. They agree to keep the house for a specified period of time—usually 5 years.

After 5 years they agree to sell the property. Out of the proceeds the uncle will first get all of his money back. Any remainder (after closing costs have been paid, of course) is usually split between home buyer and uncle.

This method, sometimes also called "sharing ownership," is helpful to the home buyer because it allows him or her to get into a property with no down payment. It is helpful to the uncle (or "aunt") because it allows him or her to get into the property with no management headaches and a percentage of the profit. Many agents are now promoting this technique as a way to buy high-priced property during a time of high interest rates.

It has its drawbacks, however.

What if the property should happen not to appreciate?

Some areas of the country are experiencing depreciation or a loss of value. In this case the uncle might not only fail to receive a profit, he or she might actually end up losing all or part of the money invested!

For the home buyer, it could be just as bad. This person would end up making house payments often far higher than he or she could have rented a comparable house for, and at the end of the term, might end up with nothing to show for it!

Potentially a far more serious problem (since there is likely to be some appreciation over 5 years) is any disagreement between uncle and home buyer. The arrangement spelling out the terms between these two parties is in the form of a contract. This contract is not part of the deed to the property nor is it part of any mortgage on it. It is separate. (The coowners do, however, usually take title to the property as "tenants-in-common.")

What this means is that should there be any disagreement between the two parties (over, for example, the ultimate selling price or arising out of the home buyer's sudden inability to make the monthly mortgage payments), the only solution might be litigation. Each party might have to hire an attorney and fight it out in court—a costly and often lengthy experience.

Some rich uncle arrangements anticipate this problem and call for mandatory arbitration. Both parties agree to waive their rights to a law suit and to abide by a prenamed arbitrator. This is not always a good idea and you should definitely consult with your attorney before signing such an agreement.

The "rich uncle" arrangement is a way to buy property using creative financing. But, like other ways, it too has its problems.

RENTING TO OWN

Finally, some buyers today have come up with what is a fascinating way for buying property. They rent.

What they do is to rent a piece of property on a long-term lease. Then they take out an option to buy the property at some future date. With the rental agreement, they obtain a fixed monthly payment often far lower than they would have to pay if they mortgaged the property on a normal purchase. With the option they lock in a price. Presumably when the property appreciates several years down the road, they'll exercise the option and buy at yesterday's price.

For the buyer the advantages here are great. But, there are also problems. One problem is that there is no clear title given. The lease and the option are basically contracts. While they affect the title, they do not clearly convey it. If the seller at some point down the road, refuses to honor either of them, litigation is often the only answer for the buyer.

For the seller the only advantage is getting rid of the property. But, the disadvantages are enormous. Instead of selling, the seller ends up tying up the property for years. In addition, the seller agrees to sell at today's price, years into the future—simply a ridiculous commitment. And what's possibly most hazardous, in order to get some cash out of the deal for the seller, a new hard money second is often put on the property with the buyer agreeing to make a monthly payment sufficient to cover all mortgage, taxes, and insurance. But, if a few months down the road the buyer can't make the payments, the seller is left still holding the house. Only now it has a new big mortgage on it.

"Renting to buy" and the "rich uncle" are two largely untried techniques: they have never been used on a large scale over a period of years. In a sense they are like taking an unproven drug. While it may accomplish the goals set out for it, it may also have unexpected side effects that could kill the patient. This is not to say that you shouldn't consider them or that they won't work. Only that my suggestion is that you first consult with a trusted attorney or a real estate broker who has had some experience with them, both good and bad.

CREATIVE FINANCING AS A SOLUTION

We've covered a number of methods of creative financing. But, in reality, we've only scratched the surface. There are hundreds of variations on the techniques discussed and many other techniques yet to be considered. What's important to understand is that creative financing is a mixed blessing. It can, of course, have drawbacks and be abused. But, it can also mean a good sale where a sale is not possible any other way. Creative financing is not a devil by any means. But, then again, it's not an angel either.

SEVEN

Private Mortgage Insurance —How to Get 5 Percent Down Without Creative Financing

Getting the down payment as low as possible has become a necessity for many buyers today. With prices so high, few people have the resources for a big down, particularly first-time buyers. For a $60,000 home, a typical 20 percent down payment is $12,000. When closing costs are thrown in, the new buyer may have to come up with $14,000 or more, just to get in. That's a lot of cash.

Of course, in our chapters on creative financing and government mortgages, we saw how it was possible to reduce the down payment, even get in for nothing down. But, many buyers and sellers do not want to use these techniques (or cannot use them). What is left for them? Are they out in the cold?

Not at all. There is a feature which can be added to virtually any institutional mortgage whether it be fixed-rate, GPM, ARM, SAM or whatever, that can increase the mortgage amount to 95 percent of the house value—all without either FHA/VA or creative financing. In fact, it's done all the time by most lenders.

PRIVATE MORTGAGE INSURANCE

What we're talking about is something called private mortgage insurance (PMI). It's both old and new.

Private mortgage insurance companies have been around virtually since before the turn of the century, although they actually became fully legal in 1911. They were widespread during the 1920s, but their collapse during the depression led both the public and the financial community away from them. It wasn't until the mid-1950s when a new company, the Mortgage Guarantee Insurance Corporation (MGIC), came into existence, that the field was revitalized. Today there are a dozen PMI companies across the country handling billions of dollars of business each year.

What Is a PMI?

Private mortgage insurance is extraordinarily simple. It is exactly what it says it is. First of all, it's an insurance plan. It insures the person or company which lends money on a mortgage against loss. What makes PMIs so unusual is that the insurer is not the government, as is the case with FHA mortgages, but rather is a private insurance company. And there you have it—private mortgage insurance.

How Does a PMI Work?

The operation of a PMI is easy to understand. It works almost exactly the same way as FHA insurance works. The private insurance company insures the lenders against loss for the top 20 to 25 percent of the mortgage (the lender's option).

If, for example, we have a mortgage for $60,000 which has 25 percent PMI on it, what is the amount of the insurance? The amount is 25 percent of $60,000, or $15,000. What's critical to the lender, however, is that it's the *top* $15,000. In the event the borrower got into trouble, there was a foreclosure and a loss on the property, the first $15,000 of the loss would be insured *to the lender*. Let's say that, at a foreclosure sale, the property only brought $45,000. How much money would the lender who held a $60,000 mortgage lose?

With a PMI on the property, the lender would lose nothing. The insurance company would make good the first $15,000. In this case that was the total shortage. The lender would get $45,000 from the sale and $15,000 from the insurer equaling the $60,000 mortgage liability.

On the other hand, if the property only brought $40,000, the lender would lose $5,000.

$60,000		Money loaned
	$40,000	From sale of property
	+15,000	Maximum insurance
−55,000	$55,000	Lender's return
5,000		Lender's loss

The Insurance Premium

Of course, the private mortgage insurance company doesn't insure mortgages for nothing. It charges a fee. That fee varies between ¼ and ½ percent (normally it is ¼ percent). That amount is added to the mortgage interest rate and is paid by the borrower. (If the mortgage interest rate were 14 percent, with PMI insurance at ¼ percent, the borrower would pay at 14¼ percent.) It works in exactly the same way as FHA insurance works.

Why would a borrower want to bother with PMI? After all, if you're going to have to pay 14 percent interest already, why would you want to increase that amount by another ¼ percent? It's like the straw that could break your back.

The answer has to do with lowering the down payment. PMI insurance allows the lender to lower the down payment to as little as 5 percent, and to get that low down, most borrowers are willing to pay the cost in the form of ¼ percent added interest.

How PMIs Lower the Down Payment

Virtually all lenders (banks, savings and loans, and so on) are allowed by their federal regulators to grant mortgages of up to 80 percent of the market value of the property. The federal regulators feel that the lenders must maintain at least a 20 percent margin for safety (in case they have to take back the property in a foreclosure).

This 80 percent rule is somewhere written in stone. If one of the lenders offers more (beyond a certain percentage of assets), it sets up a red flag, and investigators from federal agencies descend to see what's going on.

However, the 80 percent rule can be changed provided the lender can show the regulating agencies that it has adequate protection for the amount it has loaned above 80 percent. How does the lender do this? It obtains mortgage insurance. It is possible for the lender to obtain mortgage insurance for mortgages of up to 95 percent of the market value of the property.

Lenders, therefore, can easily make 95 percent mortgages.

Of course, as in most things in life there's a catch. There are two here.

The first limitation is that most lenders may not make more than 5 or 10 percent of all their loans in the 95 percent category. That means that, for every mortgage offered at 95 percent of market value, another 19 must be offered at 80 or 90 percent of value. The lenders simply don't have all that much money to spread around at 95 percent.

The second limitation is that it is hard for the borrower and property to qualify at 95 percent.

QUALIFYING FOR A PMI

In order to get a mortgage from a lender, a borrower has to meet that lender's qualifications. In earlier chapters we suggested what those qualifications typically are.

In order for a borrower to get a 95 percent mortgage, he or she must meet not only the lender's qualifications, but the insurer's qualifications as well. The process is not lengthy nor complicated, but it is strict.

Normally the PMI company accepts all the information directly from the lender. It looks at the standard forms that the borrower has filled out giving credit history, income, assets, property appraisal, and so forth.

The difference is that whereas, a lender might be willing to offer a mortgage at 30 to 35 percent debt ratio (the ratio of debt to income—see page 168), a PMI company might only be willing to accept a 25 to 29 percent ratio. Where a lender might be willing to excuse a couple of late payments on a borrower's credit history, the PMI company might not. The difference is that the PMI company has to watch out for its own shirt. It's sticking its neck out and insuring the most vulnerable part of the mortgage—the first 20 or 25 percent. It wants to be very sure that the borrower is not only a good, but a great, credit risk. The same holds true with regard to the condition and location of the property.

In order to get PMI, you have to be an outstanding borrower buying an outstanding house. In order to qualify for this 5 percent down feature, you must have strong income and strong credit.

WHY LENDERS LIKE PMIs—THE SECONDARY MORTGAGE MARKET

Many borrowers do qualify for PMI mortgages. And lenders like to give them. They particularly like 90 percent PMIs, but they also don't mind 95 percent mortages, when they are able to offer them.

One big reason that PMIs are so appealing to lenders has to do with the secondary mortgage market.

As we've seen in several places in this book, there is a thriving secondary mortgage market. It buys mortgages from the primary lenders. It, so to speak "cashes them out," and often leaves them with a profit. Lenders usually want to be sure that they can sell a mortgage in this secondary market.

There are basically three elements to the secondary mortgage market:

Fannie Mae

The largest purchaser of mortgages from lenders is the Federal National Mortgage Association (FNMA—Fannie Mae). It was born in the 1930s and has a portfolio of over $50 billion dollars, making it the fifth largest corporation in the country in terms of assets. It buys mortgages from lenders who have first made them to borrower/buyers. Ninety percent of its mortgages are FHA/VAs.

Freddie Mac

The Federal Home Loan Mortgage Corporation (FHLMC—Freddie Mac, also known as the Mortgage Corporation) is perhaps the second largest secondary buyer. It purchases well over $2 billion in mortgages each year. It primarily buys conventional or nongovernment-backed mortgages.

Ginnie Mae

The Government National Mortgage Association (GNMA—Ginnie

Mae) buys mortgages from institutional lenders and packages them for resale to investors.

Of primary interest to us are Fannie Mae and Freddie Mac. Lenders for profit and for liquidity reasons want to know that either they can immediately sell mortgages to these organizations or that at some point later in time they can sell them. Being able to sell a mortgage in the secondary market is of vital importance to most lenders.

Before a lender can sell a mortgage to the two primary buyers—Fannie Mae and Freddie Mac—that mortgage must have private mortgage insurance (or be government guaranteed or insured).

It's as simple as that. In order to dump the loan to the major buyers in the secondary market, the mortgage has to have a PMI.

Lenders, therefore, are most anxious to have mortgages with PMIs on them. You don't have to talk a lender into putting private mortgage insurance on a mortgage. (In most cases you have to talk a lender out of it, if for some reason you don't want it.)

GETTING RID OF THE INSURANCE PREMIUM

There's one additional point which should be noted about PMIs from the borrower's viewpoint. Once we obtain a PMI, we end up paying ¼ percent more per month on our mortgage. As we noted earlier, if our mortgage interest rate happens to be 14 percent, with the PMI it becomes 14¼ percent.

What happens after we've been paying on this mortgage for a number of years and have paid it down somewhat?

The private mortgage insurance only covers the top 20 or 25 percent of the mortgage amount. If we originally took out a mortgage for 95 percent of the value of the property, which had 20 percent PMI coverage, and we've paid that mortgage down to 75 percent of the original value, can we get the PMI removed?

Yes, we can.

Normally, once we've paid a mortgage down to about 80 percent of the original value (the appraised market value at the time the mortgage was placed on the property), we can request our lender to remove the private mortgage insurance. Most lenders will quickly comply.

The reason we would want to do this is to save that extra ¼ percent we've been paying every month. On a $60,000 mortgage, a ¼ percent per month can come to about $12 cash per month. That $12 is far better in our pockets than in the insurance company's pockets.

APPRECIATION DOESN'T REDUCE PMI COVERAGE

This raises an interesting question. In recent years the value of homes has skyrocketed. A person who obtained a home with a $60,000 mortgage for 95 percent of the value back in 1975 probably finds that the home today might be worth $125,000. Even though the mortgage may not have been paid down to 80 percent of the *original* appraised valued, the house has gone up in price to the point where perhaps the mortgage value realistically today is only half of the market value. Can the PMI be removed on the basis that the house is worth much more than the required 20 percent margin?

In most cases, no.

Realistically there is no reason to continue on with private mortgage insurance if we have a mortgage that is 80 percent or less of the true market value. But, rules are rules, and the current appraised value doesn't seem to have any influence here. It's the original appraised value that the lender, the insurance company, and the secondary lender go by.

It's not hard finding a lender willing to make 95 percent mortgages. Banks, savings and loans, and others through mortgage bankers will do it. Private mortgage insurance is the answer.

The difficulty is in being a strong enough buyer to qualify. In today's market, if interest rates zoom up to 16 percent, it's tough to qualify. Throw another ¼ percent for mortgage insurance on the top and it could be impossible.

Private mortgage insurance can help. But, if it doesn't, consider the other chapters on creative financing and government-backed mortgages.

EIGHT

Three Creative Mortgage Plans —Land Leases, Municipals, and Reverse Annuities

LAND LEASE—USING A COMMERCIAL ANSWER FOR HOUSES

If you own a business and you need a building out of which to operate, but you can't afford to spend any cash to acquire it, what do you do?

The answer is old and traditional. You lease land from a landowner (saving you the costs of purchase) and then you borrow money on a mortgage to put up a building. Your out-of-pocket costs have been low. You didn't have to put up a big down payment for the land, since you don't own it. And you didn't have to pay for the building, since you mortgaged it.

There's an additional bonus. Your land rental costs are probably less than your mortgage costs, so overall, you are paying *less* per month than if you had gone out and bought property and then built on it.

The land lease has allowed you to come in with little or nothing down and reduce your monthly payments.

It's done every day in commercial and industrial properties.

So, some enterprising real estate entrepreneurs have asked, why can't it also be done with residential properties? In times of high interest rates and high prices, why can't buyers use land-lease techniques to lower the down and the monthly payments? It would allow them to get into property they couldn't otherwise afford. It would allow them to obtain property in a far more reasonable fashion.

Land Leasing in the Past

While land leasing of homes may sound totally foreign to us, there is precedent for it. In Hawaii, 48.5 percent of the land is owned by the state. About 40 percent of the balance is still controlled by large estates dating back to the days of the great kings of the islands. In Hawaii most of the homes are sold under land leases. It has become the conventional way of doing things.

The same holds true in Palm Springs, California. There, back in 1876, President Ulysses S. Grant gave the land to the Ague Caliente bands of the Cahuilla Indian tribe. A century later when the white man wanted to settle in the area, the tribe didn't sell its land, it leased it. Most of Palm Springs is land leased from the Indians.

Land Leasing Today

In today's market place, many builders/developers are resorting to the land lease in an attempt to sell their vacant homes. They've found that frequently they can reduce a normal $20,000 down payment to $5000 or less. And a $1500-a-month payment can be cut down to the range of $1000 a month. It's terrific inducement for the home buyer. And home buyers have been taking advantage of it.

Even some savvy individual home sellers have been catching on to the potential of land leases. They have been selling their houses in this fashion. The advantages for the buyer are obvious (low down, low payments). For the seller the advantages are a quicker sale and sometimes more money at the end of the deal.

If land leases sound like an exciting option, that's because they are. But, they're not for everyone. Not every piece of property is suited to it nor every buyer and seller. And, as we'll see later, there are major problems.

How a Land Lease Works

In the traditional structuring of a real estate deal, the buyer purchases both the land and the improvements on it. The buyer obtains the highest form of title known as "fee simple."

In a land lease, the buyer obtains a lower form of title. The buyer obtains a "leasehold." The concept of a leasehold is quite old. In ancient times, the king or monarch would "own" all the land of the country and the people would simply work it for him. In a sense they leased it.

More recently, in England dating from the Norman conquest, leaseholds have been common. Certain families were granted large pieces of land by the crown and they in turn leased it to tenants who paid them rent. The owners became known as the "landed gentry."

In the United States, leasing is a most common practice. When an individual or family rents an apartment or house from an owner, it is most commonly one form or another of a lease.

So, the idea of leasing is nothing new. What is new to the residential field is leasing only one part of the property—the land. Under a land lease the owner typically leases just the lot. The house and improvements are sold. In this sense, the land lease is a kind of combination lease and sale.

WALKING THROUGH A LAND LEASE

Emil wanted to buy Hazel's property. She was willing to sell. But, he could not afford her price. She wanted $100,000.

Emil had only $5000 to put as a down payment and he could not qualify for a new mortgage of $95,000 (at 14 percent, his payments would have been $1125 plus taxes and insurance).

So Emil and Hazel tried some creative financing in the traditional way. She said she was willing to carry back some paper. But, she wouldn't carry it back unless Emil came up with more than $5000 as a down. She didn't want to be stuck taking money out of her pocket to pay for closing costs and commission (not to mention the problems that might occur if Emil was forced into default on the mortgage—see the chapter on creative financing).

Emil shook his head and said he had no more money. Besides, the most he could afford before taxes and insurance was $800 a month. It seemed there was no way out. Then Hazel contacted a friend who had sold under a land lease. After working out the details, Hazel offered Emil this deal:

Down payment—Emil could come in with just $5000 down.

Mortgage—Emil would apply for one mortgage with a value of $60,000. His payments on the mortgage would be about $700 a month.

Land lease—Emil would accept a lease on the land under the house from

Hazel for $100 per month. The initial value of the land would be set at $35,000.

Hazel's deal

$ 5,000	Down payment		
60,000	First mortgage	$ 700	Monthly
+ 35,000	Land Lease	+ 100	Monthly
$100,000	Total price	$ 800	Total monthly

Emil read the deal over several times, then asked, "Is it so simple? Will I really own the property?"

Hazel smiled, "Not exactly. You'll have a leasehold interest in it. The way I have it set up is that, if you want to convert your leasehold into full ownership (fee simple), you can convert by paying off the lease—initially $35,000. That will give you full ownership. You'll have the option of doing that at any time during the 30 years the lease is to run."

"I'll have a lease for 30 years?"

"That's correct," Hazel continued. "In addition, the amount of money that you owe on the lease will go up. It will be tied to the Consumer Price Index. If the CPI goes up 10 percent next year, at the end of that year you'll owe 10 percent, or $3500, more (for a total of $38,500), and so on.

"In addition, your monthly payments will also go up on the lease. Although they will only be $100 the first year, they will jump to $150 the second and $200 the third. They will continue on up by $50 a month each year."

Emil looked shocked. "That means that by year five I could be paying $300 a month on the lease alone!"

"Correct," Hazel said. "However, I don't expect that by year five you will still have the lease. I expect that by then you will either have refinanced the property or sold. You see, my goal is to get my money out. I'm not interested in indefinitely leasing the property. I'm interested in selling. What I'm doing through this land lease is giving you some time. During this time you can increase your income, wait for better financing to come along, or sell at a profit.

"Or, if you so desire, you could always keep the lease indefinitely. But, it becomes more and more expensive to keep."

Emil nodded. He understood. It was a gamble for him. But, he understood and he accepted the deal.

TIME BUYING

Hazel's deal with Emil is typical of the kind of residential land leasing that's beginning to occur in various places around the country. It is essentially a kind of "time buying." The buyer can't really afford the property today. So, the seller makes it possible for the buyer to get in on the assumption that he or she will be able to afford it some time in the future. Let's look at the deal's advantages from Hazel's viewpoint.

Advantages for Hazel

1. She was able to sell her property.

2. She had a secure sale. Even though Emil only put $5000 down, the $35,000 value of the lease was still in Hazel's name. She owned the land. If Emil couldn't keep up the payments and she were forced to foreclose, she would take back a property with only a $60,000 mortgage on it—when the value was $100,000 (established by the sales price).

3. On the $35,000 she in effect loaned to Emil, she was getting an excellent rate of return. First, it was tied to an inflation index. That meant that the value of the land increased according to inflation. (There was no loss on her money due to a loss in value of the dollar.) If inflation were 10 percent a year for 3 years, Hazel's land lease at the end of that time would be worth $42,350. That's the amount that Emil would owe her. (It could be more or less depending on the actual inflation, of course.)

In addition, there was the monthly payment. The first year she was getting $100 a month, or $1200 a year. That comes to a "real" rate of return (we've just seen it's been adjusted for inflation) of 3.5 percent. Here's how her return looks after 3 years.

RETURN ON $35,000 FOR 3 YEARS

Year one	***Real Rate of Return (after inflation), %***
1	3.4
2	4.7
3	5.6

If these interest rates look small, it must be remembered that they are after an increase has been made to the principal for inflation. (Reread the paragraphs above.) If inflation were 10 percent per year, each of these would be increased by 10 percent. Suddenly, the interest-rate return looks much better.

The advantages for Emil on this deal are also great.

Emil's Advantages

1. He buys a $100,000 home with only $5000 down—this in the face of the fact that he can't qualify for an institutional 95 percent mortgage.

2. His payments for the first year, mortgage and lease combined, are only $800 a month. (Of course, if he secures an ARM, this could vary.)

3. There's no question of qualifying.

4. After a few years he hopes to refinance out or sell. It's a perfect deal for all concerned, right?

Maybe.

As I indicated at the onset, the land lease is a creative solution to financing that will work in some cases. But, in many cases it may simply not be suited to the deal. Let's go back and take another look at Hazel's property, this time from the viewpoint of the existing financing. From this, perhaps we can come to a deeper understanding of the limitations of the land lease.

Hazel's Original Financing

Hazel had purchased her property in the conventional manner. She had taken out a first mortgage and paid cash down on it. She had bought 5 years earlier for $50,000. Her mortgage was $40,000. At the time of the sale, the remaining mortgage balance was about $48,000.

When Emil bought, he obtained a new mortgage for $60,000 plus gave Hazel $5000 in cash. This she used to pay off her existing mortgage and get cash out herself.

Hazel's Financing at Time of Sale

$ 5,000	Down payment
60,000	Emil's new mortgage
65,000	Total cash
– 48,000	Payoff of existing mortgage
17,000	Cash to Hazel
– 10,000	Costs of sale including commission
$ 7,000	Net cash to Hazel

Hazel got $7000 immediately. She also got a land lease for $35,000 and, since she had originally been willing to carry the financing, this wasn't a hardship.

What's important to see is that the deal could only be made because Hazel had a large enough equity in the property to both pay off the existing mortgage and carry the lease herself.

If Hazel, for example, owed $55,000 or more on her existing mortgage, the deal couldn't have been made. There simply wouldn't have been enough equity to pay off the old mortgage and the closing costs, and give a $35,000 land lease.

For a land lease to work, the seller has to have sufficient equity in the property to cover the value of the land.

The $35,000 figure for the land that Hazel used was a true estimate. On a $100,000 piece of property in her area, she figured that the land value was indeed 35 percent. The lender who gave Emil his $60,000 mortgage agreed. Remember, the lender is primarily loaning on the value of the improvements.

While the lender may indeed be willing to loan $95,000 on the sale of a $100,000 piece of property, land *and* house, that same lender may be willing to only lend a maximum of $60,000 on a land lease only. When the building is the main form of collateral, then the value of the building counts principally in calculating the loan amount.

DISADVANTAGES OF THE LAND LEASE

As we've seen, one of the biggest problems with the land lease is simply that most sellers probably can't afford to handle it.

There are a few more disadvantages of the land lease that should be noted.

Disadvantages for Hazel

1. In order for Emil to secure the mortgage on the property, it will probably be necessary for Hazel to agree to give a lease for at least as long a term as the mortgage will run. If it's a 30-year mortgage, that's a 30-year lease. A 40-year mortgage would require a 40-year lease. That's a long time to string out the repayment on a house sale.

2. Most lenders will require that Hazel enter into the mortgage along with Emil. That means that, in the event Emil doesn't pay on the mortgage, Hazel will be responsible for payment.

3. If Emil goes into default on the mortgage, Hazel will have to pick it up. That means her lease will need to contain a clause allowing her to do this. This is complicated language and requires the aid of a good attorney in its preparation.

4. If Emil pays on the mortgage, but refuses to pay her on the lease, she could be in real trouble in some areas. Certain states prevent the lessor (landlord) from immediately reclaiming the property from a lessee (tenant) who does not pay promptly. In some cases, the lessor may only recover the money as it is due. That means that Hazel might only be able to recover her $100 a month or $150 a month or whatever, by suing each month as it came due (or waiting until the lease term was up and suing for the whole amount).

The point here is that a lease is a difficult animal and it can conceivably cause problems for the landlord. It shouldn't be entered into lightly without good legal advice.

Disadvantages for Emil

For Emil there are also disadvantages.

1. If Emil wants to sell the property, chances are he's going to have to first pay off Hazel. That means he won't be able to offer creative financing to a potential new buyer. Rather, he will need to find a buyer with all cash to the seller. That's a decided drawback.

2. If Emil can't resell and if for any reason he can't refinance, in a few years

his lease payments are going to become an incredible burden. Going up by $50 a year, at the end of year ten he'll owe $550 a month on the lease alone. In addition, since the lease amount goes up with inflation (yet property values may not), it is conceivable that after a long number of years, he could owe more on the combined lease and mortgage than the value of the property!

3. Normally Emil can deduct a large portion of his house payment on his income taxes. All that portion which goes to interest is normally deductible.

But, under the land lease, much less goes to interest while much more goes to pay the lease. In our example, the $100 that Emil paid per month on his lease probably would not be deductible. On the other hand, if that $100 were paid toward mortgage interest it would.

One of the problems for Emil is that, from a tax viewpoint, it's costing him more to lease than to buy outright. (This is different for business. Businesses may usually deduct the lease payments as a legitimate business expense. The homeowner probably cannot.)

Of course, there are other concerns with a land lease. Once again, I emphasize that one should never enter into it without first consulting an attorney.

As an exotic form of financing, land leases are beginning to spread across the country. Individual land-lease sales are still few and far between as of this writing. But, builder land-lease sales are growing by leaps and bounds, particularly in southern California, where several major construction firms have been offering them regularly as a means of quickly selling their property.

The land lease—an exotic, but important option for both buyer and seller.

MUNICIPAL MORTGAGES

A new kind of lender has come onto the scene in the past few years—one which brings with it a big advantage that is passed on to the consumer.

How would you like a mortgage at 9 percent, when the current mortgage interest rate is 15 percent? How would you like the interest rate on that mortgage to be *fixed* for 30 years?

If it sounds too good to be true, it almost is. Yet, this is the kind of financing that municipal mortgages have offered to borrowers.

What Is a Municipal Mortgage?

A municipal mortgage is simply the old fixed-rate or adjustible-rate mortgage we have already discussed. In form it is identical to these.

What is unique about this mortgage is the lender. Rather than a bank or a savings and loan association or even an insurance company, it is usually a city, a county, or even a state. A branch of local government is the lender, hence the term "municipal" mortgage. (In some localities they are also known as tax-exempt bond mortgages.)

How Does It Work?

A municipal works quite simply. The local government agency is allowed to sell tax-exempt bonds in the general bond market. These are simply bonds like any other, with one big, important exception—the person who buys the bond does not have to pay federal income tax on the interest.

That means that someone who buys the bond will receive tax-free income. The result of this is that the government agency selling the bond can offer it at a much lower than market interest rate.

Perhaps how this works can best be seen from an example. Heloise is in the 50 percent tax bracket. She pays 50 percent of her income to the federal government in taxes. If she buys a conventional bond on which the interest is $10,000, half goes in taxes.

$10,000	Interest from bond
× 50%	Tax bracket
$ 5,000	Amount paid in taxes

But, now let's say that Heloise can buy a tax-exempt bond. On this bond she pays no taxes.

$ 5,000	Interest from bond
− 0	Taxes
$ 5,000	Amount of income kept

Note that in Heloise's tax bracket, she ends up with the same income kept whether the bond produces $10,000 regularly or $5000 tax exempt. What does that mean for the issuer of the bond?

For the local government agency, it means that it can offer to pay a far lower interest rate on its tax-exempt bond, yet still give the same rate of return to the buyer. It means that tax-exempt bonds carry much lower interest rates than regular bonds.

Municipal Bonds Make for Municipal Mortgages

The idea is this: Why not use the city's ability to issue tax-free bonds at low interest rates? Then, once the money is obtained at interest rates close to half the going market rate, why not turn around and offer it as mortgages to home buyers at the same lower rate?

The home buyers would put up their property as collateral, just as is normally done. The mortgage instruments would be the same. The only difference would be that the lender, because of its ability to issue tax-free bonds, could obtain money at far below market rates. And it could then pass these savings along to the home buyer.

A perfect idea?

For many home buyers it certainly is.

Restrictions on Municipals

The biggest problem with the municipal mortgage is the government. Washington feels that there is no such thing as a free lunch. The tax-exempt feature doesn't mean that no one pays for the interest-rate differential—it means that the federal government pays in the form of lost income-tax revenues.

In 1980, Congress approved restrictions on municipal bonds in the Mortgage Subsidy Bond Tax Act. That effectively closed down the municipal mortgage.

But, in 1981, the Treasury lifted the ban on municipals, with certain restrictions:

1. No state can issue more than $200 million of the mortgages or 9 percent of the total principal amount of mortgages issued in the state in the previous 3 years. This will effectively limit the number of municipals available to between $10 and $15 billion per year.

2. The borrower *must* intend to live in the home being purchased.

3. Mobile homes are not eligible.

4. Only first-time home buyers may obtain a municipal. If you've owned a home in the previous 3 years, you may not get a municipal. (There is an

exemption here for those who live in certain economically distressed areas.)

5. The price of the home must be no more than 90 percent of the average purchase price for a single-family home in the surrounding area. (This figure is 110 percent in economically distressed areas.)

6. The interest rate on the mortgage must be no more than one percent above the interest rate on the bond. (If the bond is 9 percent, the mortgage rate would be 10 percent.)

7. Authority to issue such bonds expires on December 31, 1983.

The municipal mortgage may be the very best deal in town, if you can qualify. Unfortunately, most buyers simply cannot qualify.

If you think you can, then your best bet is to contact your local or state housing authority. In almost all cases, these mortgages are not handled through the conventional mortgage market such as through savings and loan or mortgage brokers. They are handled directly by the local government agency.

REVERSE-ANNUITY MORTGAGE

There is a totally different mortgage challenge today being faced by millions of older Americans. These are the people who no longer are working, but have retired, many on fixed incomes. They are finding it increasingly difficult to cope with inflation.

Many of these people find that the major asset they have is their home, often paid off. When they need more money, what they need to do is tap their property. That's where they can get money.

But, to tap a home for money usually means selling it. If an older person sells his or her home to get money, where is he or she to go? Usually such people are in a terrible position when it comes to having to buy or even rent new property. (If you or someone you know is faced by this problem I suggest "*The $125,000 Decision—The Older American's Guide to Selling a Home and Choosing Retirement Housing,*" McGraw-Hill, 1981.)

Another possibility is refinancing. But that presents its own problems. Older people usually need a certain amount of extra money per month on which to live. But, refinancing usually gives them a big bunch of money all at once.

Of course, they could just spend the refinanced money gradually—a little at a time. But, too often clever schemers have found ways of cheating innocent people out of their accumulated cash. And there's always the temptation to spend too much if we have a big bank account.

Helping Solve the Older American's Money Problem

A relatively new kind of mortgage is available today which attempts to solve the problem of getting increased monthly income for older Americans. It's the reverse-annuity mortgage. (But, it has one enormous drawback, which we'll see later.)

In the reverse-annuity mortgage, the borrower does not get all the money borrowed at one time. Rather, it is doled out monthly. In addition, there is no monthly payback. It works like this.

Sophie needed a reverse-annuity mortgage. She had a home worth $100,000 free and clear. So she arranged for a $50,000 reverse annuity with her banker.

The mortgage was an ARM, so it had a floating interest rate. And it was only for 10 years. It was set up so that, from the mortgage, Sophie would receive $200 per month for 10 years.

She would only be charged interest on the money she had actually borrowed. For example, after three months, she would only be charged interest on $200 times three, or $600. The interest charges would accumulate along with the principal borrowed in a mortgage fund that had been set up for her. They would increase and become an increasing liability on her property. At the end of 10 years, she would owe approximately $50,000 (principal and interest) to the bank.

At the end of the 10-year period, Sophie could either sell or refinance the house to pay off the mortgage. Or, assuming her property had appreciated, take out a new reverse-annuity mortgage, probably for another $50,000. The process could be continued indefinitely.

What happens in the reverse annuity is just the opposite from what happens with a conventional mortgage. Conventionally, you get the money first, then pay it back monthly. Here you get the money monthly and pay it back all at once.

Reverse-annuity mortgages have many advantages for older

Americans, as we've just seen. But, they also have a drawback that isn't readily visible. It's called interest on interest.

The Big Drawback

As we saw in Chapter 5 on negative amortization, when interest is added to principal, the borrower begins paying compounded interest, or interest on interest. The same happens with the reverse-annuity mortgage. Sophie essentially borrows $200 the first month. If her interest rate is 10 percent annually, her monthly interest on that money is about $1.67. The second month she borrows another $200. Does she now owe $400? No. She now owes $401.67. The interest has been added to the principal. When we calculate the interest charge in month two, we base it not only on the principal outstanding, but on the interest outstanding as well.

While this is not much of a problem initially (after all, her first month's interest is less than $2), it gets to be a big problem as the outstanding balance increases. In the last month she may owe $48,000. The interest on that amount at 10 percent a year is $400 a month. Although she is only taking out $200 a month on principal, she is accumulating interest debt at an additional $400-a-month rate.

From this viewpoint, a reverse-annuity mortgage might be viewed as a "soak-the-old" scheme.

Historically and biblically, charging interest on interest has long been considered usurious—an unconscionable and exhorbitant charge of interest. Thirty states have had usury laws specifically prohibiting interest-on-interest charges. (Although these may be preempted by federal laws allowing it.)

Should You Get a Reverse-Annuity Mortgage?

Because of their interest-on-interest feature, are these mortgages all bad?

Not necessarily. It depends on the borrower. If this is the most practical way of handling the finances for the older person, particularly when the choice may be risking loss through careless spending, perhaps it is best.

The reverse-annuity mortgage does, after all, allow the borrower to retain possession of the property. And, there is no interest until the money has first been borrowed.

The reverse annuity mortgage poses tough questions both economic and moral for both the lender and the borrower. It should never be obtained without first having a competent financial advisor examine the entire estate of the borrower as well as having both the mental and physical health of the borrower taken into consideration.

NINE

Fannie Mae Rollovers

What's the fifth largest company in the United States?

Most people when asked this question would go down the list of companies that are well known for their size—General Motors, U.S. Steel, the oil companies, and so on. It's most unlikely, however, that nearly anyone would list the fifth or even the five hundredth largest company as Fannie Mae.

WHAT IS FANNIE MAE?

Fannie Mae is short for the Federal National Mortgage Association and it has as its assets some $56 billion in mortgages. That's what qualifies it to be the fifth largest company, in terms of assets, in the country.

Fannie Mae is a mortgage company. But, at least until recently, it never talked with or did business with any actual borrowers. It was involved strictly in the secondary market.

Born in 1938 during the tail end of the depression, Fannie Mae was originally a government agency designed to help spread FHA and GI loans. It did this by creating a secondary market.

A bank would make an FHA mortgage directly to a borrower on a home, then, later, if that bank needed to quickly get its money back from the mortgage to pay borrowers (if it got into a liquidity squeeze), it could sell its mortgage to Fannie Mae. Fannie Mae would pay cash and then go on to collect the interest. It was kind of a lender's lender.

Things went well for years with Fannie Mae acting as a secondary lender to savings institutions for FHA and GI loans and then, after 1970, for certain types of traditional loans (those which didn't have

FHA or Veterans Administration backing). By 1980, more than 19 percent of Fannie Mae's portfolio was in the nongovernment loan area.

WHAT FANNIE MAE OFFERS

All this may be well and good and a nice bit of background information, but I'm sure that anyone reading this book and hungrily looking for a way to get financing is wondering what I'm leading up to.

What I'm getting at is that, within the last few years, Fannie Mae has become virtually a direct lender in certain special cases. You may be able to secure a Fannie Mae loan for below market interest rates at better than market terms. Now, I bet you'll read on!

Fannie Mae's Problems—Your Benefits

Late in the 1960s, Fannie Mae was transformed from a government agency to a quasi-private corporation. Of the 15 members of its board, 5 are still appointed by the President of the United States. It can't take any action without the approval of the department of Housing and Urban Development. All of which is to say that if it looked as though Chrysler, Ford, and General Motors had trouble transitioning into the new economics of the 1980s, they were moving like jet planes compared to Fannie Mae. Bogged down in red tape, it continued on with business as usual—until 1981.

Then in 1981, Fannie Mae began posting losses.

Since the company is traded on the New York Stock Exchange and has over 30,000 stockholders, that was a bad sign indeed. Immediately, a new chairman and chief executive were appointed and the association was trimmed down considerably and put on a battle-ready status.

However, Fannie Mae's problems stemmed not so much from its present operations as from its past ones. Virtually all its portfolio of over $50 billion in mortgages were the old, low-interest, fixed-term mortgages of the past 30 years. That meant that Fannie Mae was getting a low rate of return. In fact, during 1981, its average mortgage yield was only about 9.5 percent. That's at a time when mortgages were bringing in between 14 and 17 percent and short-term interest rates were between 15 and 20 percent. Fannie Mae was in trouble because it had too many old-fashioned mortgages on which it wasn't making enough money.

Of course, as we've noted earlier, banks and savings and loan associations could always bail out of this situation by selling their mortgages (at discount) to secondary lenders. But, Fannie Mae is a secondary lender. So what is it to do?

One solution is to sell Fannie Mae, by means of a stock or other securities, to large investors and even the public. Such a plan is being discussed at this writing, but has not been implemented.

What is being implemented, however, is a different kind of plan, one designed to boost the yield (interest-rate return) on the old Fannie Mae mortgages.

When Tradition Didn't Pay Off

For years, Fannie Mae counted on the normal buying and selling of homes to upgrade its mortgage portfolio. When someone sold their home on which there was a Fannie Mae loan, it was paid off and the buyer obtained a new mortgage. It was the traditional way things were done. But, with high interest rates and tight money, increasingly, buyers are *assuming* old Fannie Maes. That means that the association is stuck with those old mortgages even through the sale of the home on which they were written.

Fannie Mae has reasoned, however, that if it could somehow insist on the old mortgage being paid off on sale, it could upgrade its mortgages. So Fannie Mae has begun enforcing its due-on clause, which each of its mortgages contains.

However, in over 14 states the due-on clauses have been ruled unenforceable. So what is Fannie Mae to do?

The answer is a unique approach to real estate financing that benefits both Fannie Mae and the buyer and seller of homes.

FANNIE MAE'S ROLLOVERS

If you have a home on which there is a Fannie Mae mortgage (something like 10 percent of the homes in the country do in fact qualify) and that mortgage has an old interest rate, Fannie Mae may make you the following offer:

When you sell, Fannie Mae will *increase* the value of your mortgage up to nearly $100,000, if the new buyer will assume the mortgage at a new and higher interest rate. That interest rate, however, may be as much as two to four percent *below* then-current mortgage market rates!

I suggest you reread that last paragraph as it really is a startling offer. Let's consider it slowly.

Who Has a Fannie Mae Mortgage?

No one in the past received a Fannie Mae directly. Usually what happened was that the buyer obtained an FHA or GI or a conventional loan from a bank or savings and loan association. Then, during the course of the mortgage, that lender had need of cash. So the lender *sold* the mortgage to Fannie Mae.

The lender was under no obligations to tell the borrower the loan was sold to someone else. In fact, most lenders continued to collect the mortgage payment for a fee of about ½ percent for Fannie Mae. (Many lenders originated the mortgages to sell to Fannie Mae *just* to collect this fee!)

This means that most people have no idea at all if the mortgage on their property is owned by Fannie Mae or the original lender. How do you find out?

The quickest way is usually just to call your lender. The loan officer can usually quickly tell by the numbered code on the loan if it is in the lender's own portfolio or if it has been sold to Fannie Mae. If the lender still holds it, you can stop reading this chapter. You're out of luck.

But, if the mortgage has been sold to Fannie Mae, read on.

Will Your Fannie Mae Qualify as a Rollover?

The next thing to determine is whether or not your Fannie Mae mortgage will qualify for the new "rollover," as it's called. The only way to find this out is to contact Fannie Mae. But, Fannie Mae is not really prepared to handle inquiries from ultimate borrowers. It is more prepared to handle them from the loan officers of lenders. So you can have your loan officer at the bank or savings and loan where you deal find out if Fannie Mae will roll over your loan.

Generally, Fannie Mae may roll over those mortgages which have interest rates that are lower than its average yield. For example, if Fannie Mae's yield on the average was 10 percent and you had a mortgage for 9¾, you'd probably be considered a prime candidate for a rollover.

If, however, your mortgage had a 12 percent interest rate, Fannie Mae might not be interested. Your loan officer could quickly determine this, often by just a phone call.*

If you have a low interest rate and Fannie Mae is willing to roll over, you could end up with a new interest rate of 12 to 13 percent when the market rate is 15 to 16 percent. Not a bad incentive to a buyer if you're trying to sell your home. You could also end up with more cash. Here's how:

$80,000	Sales price of home
× 80%	
64,000	Potential maximum mortgage amount
– 17,000	Existing first mortgage
$47,000	Additional monies which may be advanced by Fannie Mae

In this example, the borrower would end up with a new loan of $64,000. The old $17,000 mortgage would be paid off, and the seller would get $47,000 in cash.

As of this writing, the maximum mortgage amount from Fannie Mae under this program is $97,500, but this is subject to change (as is the entire program). To find out what is currently available, your best bet is to check with your mortgage banker.

One last point to consider is assumability. Fannie Mae doesn't want to get stuck with these new mortgages as it did with the old ones. If it raises its portfolio's average yield, for example, to 14 percent, but interest rates in general rise to 25 percent, it could be in hot water all over again.

To compensate, it is instituting a 7-year "due date" on these rollovers. This simply means that, although the mortgage payments

---

* Some loan officers will give you a blank stare when you propose this. My suggestion in case your lender has never heard of this program—or doesn't want to hear of it—is to contact a mortgage *banker.* They are listed in the Yellow Pages and will probably be able to help.

are handled as if the mortgage were to be amortized for the full 30 years, it is actually all due and payable in 7 years.

But, that's not so bad. Fannie Mae will guarantee to renew the mortgage after the 7-year period, but, at a new and presumably higher interest rate.

Fannie Mae rollovers are obviously not for everyone. They are just one more of the new mortgages available during this transition period between the world of yesterday and world of today in financing. They are another play in the new mortgage game.

TEN

FHA and VA Mortgages Today

During the 1950s and part of the 1960s, the most popular mortgages in real estate were those which came under the Federal Housing Authority (FHA) and Veterans Administration (VA) programs. In those days, it seemed that when a buyer bought a home, he or she first tried to get one of these mortgages. Only after this proved impossible would the buyer settle for a "conventional," or nongovernment, mortgage.

By the end of the 1960s and going into the 1970s, however, the desirability of these mortgages dropped considerably. Private mortgage insurance (PMI) discussed in Chapter 7, made low–down-payment conventional mortgages possible. And the bureaucratic red tape, not to mention the high cost of obtaining FHA/VA loans, made them unacceptable choices. By the end of the last decade, less than 10 percent of all home mortgages were from these government programs.

As of this writing, the FHA and VA programs are in transition. It is not clear how they will adapt to the new mortgage game of the 1980s. It may well be into the 1990s, in fact, before these programs again become carefully defined. For the present, however, they are a kind of amalgam of past programs band-aided together to meet current needs.

FHA MORTGAGES

FHA mortgages are alive and well and, if you are a buyer, you probably can get one if you and the house qualify. There are certain very good reasons why you might want such a mortgage, which we'll get into in a moment. (The advantages for the buyer have always outweighed the advantages for the seller on these mortgages.)

The FHA Programs

There have been numerous FHA programs in the past. These include the following:

TITLE II			
	203	**(b)**	Financing of one to four family dwellings
	203	**(b)**	Special financing for veterans
	207		Financing rental housing and mobile home parks
	221	**(d)**	Financing low-cost one- to four-family dwellings for displaced or moderate-income families
	222		Financing one-family homes for service personnel
	234	**(f)**	Financing condominium units
	234	**(d)**	Financing condo projects and condo conversion projects
	235		Assistance to low-income families to make home purchase by subsidizing mortgage interest payments
TITLE I			
		(b)	Financing purchase of a mobile home unit

Many of these programs have been cut or at least severely pruned back by budgetary considerations in Washington. But, the basic program, which is 203 (b), still helps finance home mortgages, and it is this program with which we'll concern ourselves in this chapter. (For more information on the other programs, consult with any lender's mortgage officer or the FHA directly in Washington, D.C. Branch offices are also in most states.)

How the FHA Works

Under section 203 (b), the FHA does not really lend anyone any mortgage money. Under this section, in fact, the FHA really isn't even in the mortgage business. To make these statements understandable, we have to go back to 1934 when the FHA was first created.

It is in the middle of the Great Depression. Unemployment is hovering around 25 percent. The economy has stabilized, but at a dreadfully low level. President Franklin Delano Roosevelt has taken office with a mandate to make things better. What is he to do?

One of the things he decides to try is to get the housing industry up off its back. With banks unable to lend money on mortgages, with them foreclosing and then trying to sell off their properties for cash, the housing market has crashed. Prices have dropped as much as 50 percent in some areas. Everything is for sale. No one wants to buy. Or more precisely, no one *can* buy.

Roosevelt and his advisers reason that, if people start buying houses, builders will go back to building them and that in turn will revitalize the housing industry putting thousands in the construction industry to work. But, to get the cycle started Roosevelt has to get people buying houses. How?

The answer is financing. The watchword of the administration in terms of housing seems to be, "Give them a *way* to buy, and they will buy."

FHA to Prosperity

The government creates the Federal Housing Administration, quickly nicknamed the FHA, and it creates something totally new in financing—the 20-year loan! Imagine how unheard of this truly was. The typical mortgage had been for 6 months or at best a year. Now, suddenly, the government is talking about 20 years. "Betting on the future," is what it is called, and it seems a real gamble from the depths of the Depression.

And if it isn't remarkable enough that the FHA is considering making loans for 20 years, what really grabs the headlines is that it's talking about a down payment of only 3 percent! On a $5000 house that's only $150! For a measly $150 a person can get into a house and then have payments extending for over 20 years.

It really was something exciting and revolutionary to people in the 1930s. Of course, you had to have a solid job to qualify for one of those newfangled FHA loans, but then roughly 50 percent of the working population did. (Remember, at its worst only 25 percent were unemployed during the Depression.)

People who had been afraid to take a chance, suddenly saw

opportunity. The housing market was depressed, prices had fallen to record low levels and now it was possible to buy some of that depressed property for almost nothing down and very little a month. "Why not take a chance?" became the watchword. "Things are so bad now, how can they get worse, and at least this is a chance for a future!"

Not everyone swarmed to the FHA loans and to buy houses. It was only a trickle at first. But the new financing was a start.

Only there was a problem, a big one for the FHA. Revenues from taxation were way down for the federal government. Not only that, but Roosevelt was planning all sorts of government-sponsored social programs like the Works Progress Administration (WPA) and the Civilian Conservation Corps (CCC) that would use government money. While the FHA got enough money to start an administration, it didn't get any money to make loans. What good was the FHA which promised these fantastic loans if it had no money to fund them?

Insured Loans

It took an unnamed genius to solve this one. Someone in the FHA came up with the brilliant idea of having the regular banks make the new mortgages, those banks that still had money. The FHA would simply guarantee the loans. Just as the new Federal Deposit Insurance Corporation (FDIC) was guaranteeing depositors against loss from banks that collapsed, the FHA would itself guarantee banks against borrowers that couldn't make their payments. The FHA would not offer loans. It would offer the only thing it had—the guarantee of the U.S. government.

Only the U.S. government's guarantee wasn't too good right then. The bankers wanted to see a little money behind that guarantee.

So, in a leap of genius, the FHA, modeling itself even more closely after the FDIC, imposed a surcharge of at first ¼ then ½ percent on mortgages the banks made. It was simple. If the banks charged 4 percent interest, the FHA would charge ½ percent extra so the borrower ended up paying 4½ percent. To the borrower, the extra ½ precent was negligible. But, to the FHA it was the difference between viability and death. With the ½ percent the FHA created a fund, a fund that could be used to pay off those mortgages that went into default.

Suddenly the bankers picked up their ears. Here was a terrific deal for them. They could lend money, and its repayment would truly be insured by a federal agency that had a fund ready to make payoffs.

And that's basically how the FHA worked back in the old days and how it still works today. Of course there have been a few changes. The interest rate which may be charged on an FHA loan and which is set by the government, has moved steadily upward over the years. (Few people can still remember the days of 4½ percent mortgages!)

And the current term for FHA mortgages is the standard 30 years.

But, other than that, the basic operation of the program is the same. The FHA is essentially a mortgage insurance company.

Advantages of the FHA

For the buyer of a home there are some decided advantages in getting an FHA loan. These include the following:

1. The interest rate is usually between ½ and 1½ percent *below* the market rate. That means that the buyer probably will end up with a better interest rate than if he or she attempted to obtain a conventional mortgage. (The New ARM may soon be accepted as FHA.)

2. FHA mortgages are *discounted* to make up for the lower-than-market interest rate. We'll cover this in more detail under disadvantages for the seller in a moment. But, for a buyer, one feature of the FHA mortgage is that the buyer cannot pay a discount of more than 1 percent (one point). (This is usually called a "loan fee.")

3. FHA mortgages are *fully assumable*. This means that if you get one, you'll have no problem turning it over to someone else when it's time to sell the property. This feature, in fact, is one of the biggest advantages to sellers. A high FHA mortgage on a home is a real plus to buyers and makes a home easier to sell. (Fannie Mae, which buys FHA in the secondary market, is trying to change this feature.)

4. There are no prepayment penalties. An FHA mortgage may be paid off in full at any time without paying a penalty.

5. Not only does the buyer have to qualify for the FHA mortgage, but the property has to qualify as well. This means something more than the house simply being appraised for enough money to warrant the mortgage. It means that the house has to qualify *structurally*. Often on FHA

mortgages, the seller will be required to bring any substandard construction up to current building standards. Any damage such as done by wind, water, termites, fungus, erosion, and so forth might also have to be corrected. When a buyer purchases a home under an FHA program, he or she has a government stamp of approval on the property. That can also be a very valuable asset.

6. The down payment for the FHA mortgages is very *low*. The actual down payment varies with the amount borrowed. For example, in the past, the maximum amount of the FHA mortgages was $60,000. The down payment was calculated in this fashion.

a. 3 percent of the first $25,000

b. 5 percent of the amount over $25,000

In the case of a maximum $60,000 mortgage, the maximum down payment might, therefore, be $2500. As can be seen, this is an extraordinarily small down payment. It would result in a mortgage of $57,500 on an appraised value of $60,000.

Of course, these figures should not be taken as the current limitations on the FHA. The government has played musical chairs every few months with the FHA program over the last several years both with regard to the maximum mortgage amount and the current FHA interest rate. If you are considering an FHA mortgage, you should first check with a lender to see what the current terms and conditions are.

Disadvantages of the FHA

There are some problems for the FHA mortgages and most of these are faced by the seller. Often, these problems are the result of the very advantages these mortgages offer the buyers.

1. Because the FHA mortgage is usually offered at below market interest rates, lenders demand a discount. The discount is determined by three factors.

a. The current short-term money market

b. The age, condition, and area of the property

c. The credit-income strength of the buyer

What this all comes down to is usually the fact that there are many "points" to pay on an FHA mortgage. (A "point" is simply a convenient term for indicating 1/100th of the mortgage amount. On a $100,000 mortgage, one point equals $1000.)

In the past, a rule of thumb has been that for each ¼ percent in interest difference between the FHA interest rate and the current mortgage market interest rate, one point was charged. If, for example, FHA mortgages were 14 percent at a time when the mortgage market was demanding 16 percent in interest, there would be eight points.*

16%	Current market rate
− 14%	FHA interest rate
2%	Differential
÷ ¼	
8	Points charged

If a person were applying for a $60,000 mortgage, and the interest rates were as indicated in our illustration above, that means that there would be 8 points, or 8 percent, of $60,000 charged as a discount.

$60,000	Mortgage amount
× 8%	Discount
$ 4,800	Discounted amount

What's critical to see here is that this $4800 cannot by law be absorbed *by the buyer.* According to the terms of an FHA mortgage, the buyer cannot pay more than one point as a "loan fee." That means that the seller must foot the cost.

Of course, many sellers have tried to avoid or split that big discount by upping the price of the property. (If the buyer pays more for the property, then the buyer is in whole or in part paying for the seller's discount.)

2. The problem with this is that the FHA requires its own *appraisal.* For a fee of usually under $100, the FHA will send its own appraiser (usually an independent appraiser working for the FHA) out to see the property. This appraiser will render an evaluation of the house. The amount of the mortgage to be insured by the FHA will then be the *lower* of either.

a. The FHA appraisal

b. The selling price

---

* The discount is for all FHA mortgages issued by the lender at the time.

Because of the FHA appraisal of the property, it is not possible for the seller to jack up the price so that the buyer will help pay for the discount. (However, the buyer can, of course, pay more than the FHA appraisal. But, that will be cash out of the buyer's pocket. The mortgage amount is a percentage of the appraised value and cannot be increased over that value regardless of how high the price goes.)

3. *Cash down* by the buyer is another requirement of the FHA program. Although the down payment may be quite small, as little as 3 percent of the purchase price at certain amounts, the buyer must come up with it in cash.

No secondary financing (no seconds) are allowed in the FHA program.

There is one exception to this and that occurs when the buyer is over the age of 62. In certain instances, borrowing from a relative or friend or other types of secondary financing are allowed.

4. *Repairs* to the property must generally be made before the sale can be consummated and the mortgage funded. This presents some special problems for the seller.

Under a conventional mortgage, in most cases the property is taken *as is* by the lender. Under the FHA, as we've seen, however, the FHA may require corrective work. Given the choice between accepting an FHA offer or waiting for another buyer to come in with a conventional offer, can be a difficult decision for a seller.

Consider: Let's say the seller accepts the FHA offer and there are thousands of dollars of corrective work to be done. If the seller does this work prior to the close of escrow and then, for any reason the buyer doesn't go through with the deal, the seller is out all the money for the corrective work. It's a real consideration when you're faced by a bill for $5000 worth of repairs *before* you can sell your house.

5. *Time and red tape* is another problem for the seller. To sell the property, the seller must obtain an FHA appraisal. That means filing an application, waiting for it to get to the FHA headquarters, and then waiting for the FHA appraiser to get out to the property. Then, there's the wait while the appraisal is issued. The total time can be as short as 3 weeks and as long as 8 or more.

(Compare this with a conventional mortgage for which the appraisal can usually be obtained in about 3 working days.)

6. *There is ½ percent interest extra* for the buyer that must be paid on the FHA mortgage. You'll recall that this is the cost of the FHA insurance. It simply is one additional item that adds to the monthly cost to the borrower.

These then are some of the pros and cons of an FHA mortgage. When you take a long hard look at the con side, it's not too hard to see why these mortgages have come into disfavor in the recent past. With conventional mortgages much easier to obtain for similar down payments during the 1970s, the FHA almost drifted into oblivion.

In the past FHA mortgages were only of the fixed-interest rate type. However, as of this writing, there is a movement to change FHA to accept the new adjustable-rate mortgages (ARMs). Very possibly by the time you read this ARMs will also be part of the FHA program.

If you're considering getting an FHA mortgage, there are a few other features that you should be aware of. Mostly these consist of the special qualifying that must be done by a borrower. (FHA qualifies borrowers more stringently than many other mortgage programs.)

Qualifying for an FHA Mortgage

Qualifying for mortgages in general is handled in detail in Chapter 11. But, for the FHA mortgage, there are certain qualifications that must be met. The FHA uses the 50 percent of "net effective monthly income" method of qualifying, *in addition* to other tests.

The 50 Percent of Net Effective Income Method

To find out whether or not a borrower qualifies, the FHA generally will require the following information:

Monthly Expenses

A. Principal

B. Interest

C. Taxes

D. Utilities (including heating and cooling expenses)

E. Maintenance and repair allowance

The cost of all these items is added up. Then to these amounts are added other fixed monthly expenses. (The fixed monthly expenses are those that the borrower has incurred—such as car payments—and which are expected to run for more than 11 months.)

Once monthly expenses are known, buyer income is determined.

Monthly Income

A. Gross income

B. Less taxes

C. Net income

Once the total monthly expenses and the net income are calculated, the following formula is used:

$$\text{If } \frac{\text{total monthly expenses}}{\text{net monthly income}} = 50 \text{ percent or less, buyer will qualify}$$

What the formula does, essentially, is demand that the housing costs and other long-term costs not exceed 50 percent of the buyer's net income.

There is another additional qualification. That is that the housing costs alone (principal, interest, taxes, utilities, maintenance, and repairs) cannot normally be more than 35 percent of the buyer's net income.

Of course, simply meeting the income and expense qualifications does not necessarily qualify a buyer. There has to be a strong credit history. The FHA, however, is sometimes willing to accept extenuating conditions for a poor credit history. For example, sickness or an accident or a lay-off some time in the past might be used to explain tardy credit performance.

FHA VA Mortgages

The FHA under section 203 (b) also has a special program for qualifying veterans. Generally, those who do qualify have spent at least 90 days of active duty in the armed services. The principal advantage of this program is that it is open to vets who may not qualify under the regular VA program. Additionally, unlike the other program, the FHA/VA may be used over and over again.

Additionally, this program offers a lower down payment than that required for the standard FHA mortgage.

To obtain an FHA/VA mortgage, the veteran needs a Certificate of

Veteran Status which may be obtained from the Veterans Administration. It is submitted as part of the FHA mortgage package.

VA-GUARANTEED MORTGAGES

The Veterans Administration program is somewhat similar to the FHA program, but there are important differences. The most obvious, of course, is that the VA program is only available to U.S. veterans. In general, for those who are in the armed forces after January 31, 1955, to qualify the veteran must have served continuously on active duty for at least 181 days. In addition, the veteran must have other than a dishonorable discharge. (Some exceptions are allowed for vets who received a service-connected disability.) Special rules apply to veterans of World War II and the Korean War.

Advantages of the VA Mortgage

The big advantage that the VA program has over the FHA and conventional mortgages is that there is *no down payment.* The borrower doesn't have to put up anything to make the purchase. (The borrower may, of course, be required to pay normal closing costs.)

Beyond the no–down-payment feature, the VA program is virtually identical, in terms of advantages, to the FHA program. The mortgages thus offered have a lower-than-market interest rate (usually the same rate as for FHA mortgages), no prepayment penalty, and easy assumptions. There are two additional advantages, one in terms of qualifying, the other in terms of no insurance payment (the FHA ½ percent), both of which we'll go into in just a moment. The disadvantages of VA loans are also similar to those for FHAs.

Literally millions of veterans have used the VA program, some who have gone back and used it many times over. Yet, as in the case of the FHA, in recent years it has not been nearly as popular as conventional mortgages. Nevertheless, for the individual who can get a VA mortgage, it is probably one of the best available.

How the VA Mortgage Works

A VA mortgage works differently from an FHA mortgage. You'll recall that with the FHA we noted that the government essentially only provided insurance. But it did not actually advance any money itself.

With VA loans, the government does not provide any insurance as well as not advancing any money. Rather it provides a *guarantee* called the veteran's "entitlement."

The amount of the guarantee or entitlement has varied over the years from as little as $4000 back in 1950, to $25,000 most recently. (Check with the VA for the current entitlement amount.) If the entitlement amount were, for example, $25,000, that would be the *maximum guarantee* the VA would make on the mortgage.

At first that may not sound like a very large amount of money. Where can you find a house today that you can buy for $25,000?

Actually, the entitlement is a lot more than it sounds like. For in the event there is a foreclosure and a loss to the lender, the VA will pay off the *first* $25,000 (if that is the entitlement). In essence, the VA is guaranteeing the top of the mortgage.

Since VA mortgages are regularly sold to the secondary mortgage market (principally Fannie Mae and Ginnie Mae) these secondary lenders have come up with a formula for the maximum loan amount. It can be four times the guarantee. If, for example, the guarantee were $25,000, then the maximum mortgage amount could be $100,000.

In such a mortgage, the VA would guarantee the first $25,000 or the amount between $100,000 and $75,000. Since this is the most vulnerable area of a mortgage (the lender almost never loses more than 10 or 15 percent of the mortgage value), the VA loan makes financial sense.

As an additional boon to the veteran, there is *no charge* for the guarantee. The government picks up the cost of the program.

Entitlement Reuse

As we've noted, over the years the amount of the entitlement has changed. In some cases, veterans used their entitlement when it was, for example, only $7500. But recently the entitlement has been $25,000. Veterans in this situation may be able to use the difference ($17,500) of entitlement that they didn't use before. (The $17,500 is the equivalent of a $70,000 mortgage.)

In addition, when a veteran sells a home on which he or she has originally obtained a VA mortgage and the buyer comes in with cash to the seller and entirely *pays off* that original VA mortgage, the veteran may apply to the VA to have his or her *full* entitlement restored! What this means is that a vet can, in theory, use VA mortgage privileges over and over again.

Personal Liability

There is a catch here that has ensnarled some veterans. As noted earlier, a VA mortgage is fully assumable. But, assumable has a different meaning to the VA than to the FHA or with conventional mortgages. Assumable means that, without a fee (other than for paper work), a new buyer who may not be a veteran can assume an existing VA mortgage without qualifying either for the lender or the VA. But, if that new buyer should at any time in the future default on the mortgage and the house be foreclosed and the VA lose any money through its guarantee program on that house, the *original* veteran borrower is *personally liable for the full loss to the VA*! It's something to keep in mind if you're thinking about selling your VA mortgage house to just anyone.

Finally, a vet may take out a VA mortgage and then sell the property to another vet who has his or her own entitlement. If the new veteran buyer is willing to put up his or her own entitlement on the old mortgage, the old veteran seller may take his or her entitlement out and then use it again to buy another house.

If the entitlement sounds like a musical chairs program, you're not far off. In the heydays of VA loans in the 1950s, I can recall that many houses were bought and sold strictly on the basis of whether they had a VA mortgage.

VA Requirements

The Veterans Administration has a number of other requirements for its mortgages:

1. The vet must buy a home of no more than four units and intend to occupy one.

2. Mobile homes and condominiums are allowed under the program.

3. New construction is excluded unless it has been specifically built under VA specifications.

4. The property must be appraised by the VA. Based on the appraisal, the VA issues a Certificate of Reasonable Value (CRV) which states the government's estimate of the fair market price. The mortgage is based on the CRV or selling price, whichever is *lower.*

   In the distant past, the veteran was specifically prohibited from paying more than the CRV for a home. But, in 1968 the government changed that regulation and determined that a vet could pay whatever price he or she agreed to, providing that:

   a. The veteran paid in cash the difference between the CRV and the selling price.
   b. The veteran signed a statement that she or he has seen the CRV and knows what it contains.

5. The veteran must qualify for the mortgage. In addition to the usual income and credit requirements, the veteran must also obtain a Certificate of Eligibility from the VA. This is the form which shows that he or she is entitled to a VA mortgage.

Earlier we noted that there was one other advantage to the VA program over the FHA, and that involved more flexible qualifying. While it's true that the veteran must qualify normally, there is also a procedure of personal appeal that does not exist for any other mortgage that I know of.

If a veteran applies for a VA mortgage and is turned down because of bad credit or low income, that veteran may often be able to personally appeal the decision to the VA. There is a hearing, and if the vet can show that he or she can and will actually make the payments, then the mortgage may be granted—even if the vet does not normally qualify under income and credit rules! (At one time I thought this was not really the case, but I've seen it happen so many times that I know it to be fact.) If you're having trouble qualifying for a VA loan because of income or credit, a personal appeal may get you everywhere.

VA AND FHA MORTGAGES

We've covered both the most popular FHA and the VA programs in some detail. But, there are several other features which are common to both and which someone who is interested in them should know.

Lenders

Both VA and FHA mortgages can be obtained from a wide variety of lenders. These include banks, savings and loan associations, and mortgage bankers.

Owner/Occupant

Both VA and FHA mortgages require that the borrower be the true owner of the property (you can't legitimately use your VA to buy a home for someone else) and plan to occupy it. You can't legitimately use a VA or FHA mortgage to buy a property for investment. Although once established, you can assume one of these mortgages with the intent of using the property as a rental.

No Age Requirements

There are no age requirements for either FHA or VA mortgages (except with regard to a person who is under legal age).

Trust Funds

Both VA and FHA mortgages require that the borrower establish an impound account. (Also called a trust-fund account.) This simply means that the borrower must pay for the taxes and insurance on the property on a monthly basis, (one-twelfth each month). The money goes into a lender's special impound account, and the lender pays the fees due at the appropriate time each year.

As we've seen, the FHA and the VA are out there ready and willing to provide mortgage aid. The real question is, will high interest rates and alternate mortgages totally supplant these government programs? Or will these government programs knock alternative mortgages out of the game?

Whatever the answer, a VA or FHA mortgage should be considered when you try to finance your next home.

ELEVEN

How to Get a Mortgage From a Lender

It's one thing to know that there's a pipeline of nearly a billion dollars a week of mortgage money available in the United States, most going to families who buy homes. It's quite something else to tap that pipeline and get some of that mortgage money for yourself.

How does the average person go about getting financing for the purchase of a home? How does the seller help the buyer find institutional money? Where do you go in today's market?

We'll answer these questions and more in this chapter. We'll cover four basic areas:

1. Credit and qualifying

2. Documents

3. Property qualifying

4. Finding the right lender

Hopefully, after you've had a chance to read through this chapter, you'll have a better idea of how to present yourself and your property to a lender. You'll have a better chance of getting the mortgage you want and need.

CREDIT AND QUALIFYING THE BUYER

In Chapter 1, we briefly discussed qualifying and talked about ratios such as "4 to 1" that lenders used to determine if a potential buyer made enough money to qualify for a mortgage. You'll recall we said that the basic formula was that, after all other long-term debt (such as car payments), the borrower should be making four times the monthly mortgage payments to qualify for a loan.

That is and yet isn't true. While the 4-to-1 formula is still used by lenders, in actual practice it tends to be put aside in favor of something called the "debt" or "debt-income" ratio.

The Income-to-Monthly-Payment Ratio

Charles found a home he wanted to buy. Through his real estate broker, he offered $100,000, the purchase contingent upon his being able to obtain a new first mortgage for $80,000. The sellers signed and the deal was made. Now, of course, Charles had to find that loan. The sellers had given him 30 days to find a lender who would commit to lend him the money.

Charles asked his broker where to get the money. His broker handed him a mimeographed list. On it were the names of eight savings and loan associations, three banks and two mortgage bankers. Behind each name was the type of mortgage they were offering and the then-current interest rate.

"Take your pick," the broker said.

At that point, Charles realized he was on his own. Somehow he had thought the agent would handle it all. Now he realized he was going to have to go out there and arrange the financing himself.*

Charles picked one of the mortgage bankers and went to her. The reason he picked the mortgage banker was because after her name was a wide variety of mortgages and interest rates. The mortgage banker was in reality a finance broker with a wide range of sources for funds.

The broker's name was Alice. After brief introductions, she said that she could quickly tell Charles whether or not he would qualify for the mortgage he wanted if he would give her some basic information. Charles sat down and nodded that he was eager to begin.

"I assume you'll be getting an 80 pecent mortgage, or $80,000. The best interest rate we have right now is 14 percent on an adjustable-rate mortgage (ARM). Your monthly payments on the payback for principal and interest will be roughly $950 per month. In

---

* Some larger real estate firms do handle financing "in house." Before agreeing to go with their financing, you should first determine that they offer competitive rates.

addition, we figure about an additional 2½ percent of the sales price for taxes and insurance, or roughly $2400 a year in this case. That works out to an additional $200 a month. Your total monthly payment will be $1150.

Monthly payment

$ 950	Principal and interest
+ 200	Taxes and insurance
$1150	Total monthly payment

Charles nodded in agreement. That's about what the broker told him he'd have to pay. He knew it would be difficult to handle that much money each month, but he loved the house and he was determined to try.

"Now, let's find out if you make enough money to qualify for this mortgage. What is your salary either weekly, monthly, or annually?"

Charles was an engineer for a micro computer company, and his annual salary was $36,000 per year.

A worried frown came over Alice's face. "The industry standard is 4 to 1. On that basis, if the monthly payment is $1150, four times that is $4600. Annualized, that comes to $55,200. That's what you should be making in order to qualify for the mortgage, in theory."

$ 1,150	Monthly payment
× 4	Qualifying ratio
4,600	
× 12	Annualized
$55,200	Required annual income

Charles was shocked. He hadn't realized he should be making so much money. "I own a second mortgage on a house left to me by my father. I get an additional $400 a month for 10 years on that. Will it help?"

Alice nodded and multiplied the $400 a month times 12, coming up with $4800. When added to his $36,000 annual income from wages, it brought his income up to $40,800. "You're up to roughly $41,000. Perhaps we can do something."

"But, I'm a long way from $55,000."

"Let's wait until we get it figured out," Alice calmed him. "The 4 to 1 is in reality just a guideline. What we are more interested in is your overall debts-to-income ratio. What I now want to know is how much you owe in long-term debt to others."

The Income-to-Debt Ratio

Charles shook his head. he didn't understand.

"How much do you owe on your car?" Alice asked.

"$150 per month."

"Do you have any outstanding loans or mortgages to any savings and loans, banks, finance companies, or individuals?"

Charles indicated he had recently taken out a bank loan to buy a stereo set, but had paid it off. He had no loans outstanding.

"What about credit cards. What is your outstanding balance on all your credit cards?"

Charles thought for a moment, then decided that he might owe perhaps $800.

"How much do you pay off each month?" Alice asked.

Charles decided that it came to about $50 per month.

Alice wanted to know if there was any other debt which Charles owed that would take more than 6 months to pay off? He shook his head.

Charles' total monthly debt

$ 150	Car payment
50	Credit cards
+ 1150	Future house payment
$ 1350	Total long-term monthly debt

"Your total long-term monthly debt comes to $1350."

"Of course, there's much more. There are utility bills, food, clothes." Charles wanted to continue, but Alice held up her hand.

"We're concerned with long-term debt. What you're speaking of is short-term or month-to-month debt. That's something different. Now, let's find out what your debt-to-income ratio is.

Alice took Charles's annual income of $40,800 and divided it by 12 to get his actual monthly income. It came to $3400. Then she divided the $3400 into the monthly payment to get a percentage ratio:

$ 1350	Total long-term monthly debt
÷ 3400	Monthly income
.397	(40 percent)

"In order to meet your long-term debts, you would need roughly 40 percent of your income." Alice shook her head. "I'm afraid I can't help you. I can get you a mortgage if your debt ratio is as high as 33 or 34 percent when there's excellent credit. But, I never got one up over 35 percent. And you're already to 40 percent."

"I really don't understand what you're saying," Charles interrupted. "What does this debt-ratio thing mean?"

Alice drew Charles a chart to help clarify (Figure 11-1).

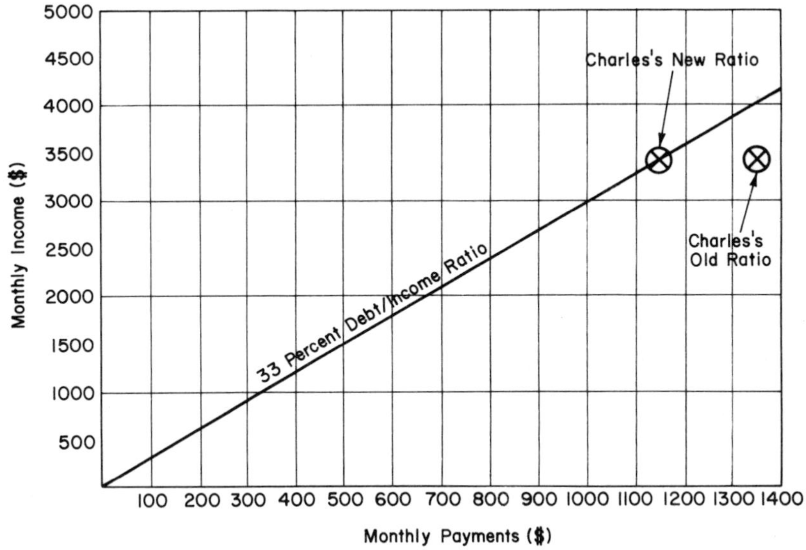

FIGURE 11–1. Debt-income ratio chart.

"On this chart, I've plotted income and monthly payments. The diagonal line indicates those points at which debt is exactly 33 percent of the monthly income—about the best ratio we can still fund a mortgage at. Next, I placed your income and debt on the chart. As you can see, you fall below the line by a considerable amount. There's no real way you can get a mortgage, given your present circumstances."

Improving Your Income-to-Debt Ratio

"What do you mean 'given my present circumstances'?"

"Well," Alice paused, "if you could either increase your income or decrease your monthly payments, it might help."

"I have $30,000 in the bank," Charles began. "I was planning to use $20,000 to put down. I could use another $2500 and pay off both the remaining car loan and the outstanding credit card debt. Would that help?"

"It might."

$ 1350	Current monthly debt (long-term)
− 200	Credit card and auto payment
$ 1150	New monthly debt

"Now your monthly debt is only $1150. Let's go back to the graph and see where it is." (See Figure 11-1.)

Alice also made the new calculation.

$ 1150	Long-term monthly debt
÷ 3400	Monthly income
.338	(34 percent)

"I think that will do it." Alice smiled. (Note: We've assumed a 34 percent ratio here. During tight money conditions, that ratio could be 30 or 29 percent or even less.)

CREDIT

In order to determine Charles' credit, Alice had him fill out two forms (sometimes combined into one).

The first form had him list any person or company he had arranged credit with during the past 10 years. This included banks and personal loans, credit cards from local department stores, gas companies and major national banks, installment loans from finance companies, mortgages on property, and so on.

"It hardly makes sense for me to list these things," Charles said. "I could only list the ones I paid back and leave off the ones I didn't pay. I could make this look as good as I liked."

Alice smiled. "The reason we have you list all these things is both for credit backgound and identification purposes. We really don't care that much which ones you put down—only that you put down enough to indicate to us two things:

1. That you have borrowed enough in the past to create a credit history

2. That we can identify you from your borrowing

"The first is more important than most people realize. It's not simply sufficient to owe nothing to anyone. That's terrible credit," Alice pointed out. "It's no credit at all. If someone comes to me and wants a mortgage and it turns out they have no credit cards, never had a bank loan, never borrowed from anyone, I can't get them a mortgage! They have no credit to check out. It's important to have borrowed sufficiently for a lender to see what your history of paying back is.

"The second reason we like to list whatever items you have borrowed from is so that when I send this form to a central credit computer, it will have something more to go on than just your name, address, and social security number. It will also have a credit history. This will help the computer identify any bad credit you may have that might not be directly linked to your name in the computer."

"You mean you don't write to each of the companies I list here?"

"I don't write to any of them. I send the form to the computer credit company. They already have data released by virtually every company you will have mentioned. They will write to those others which you put down that they don't have.

"When I get the report, it will show a series of companies from whom you've borrowed. It will indicate whether you paid the money back and if you paid it back as agreed upon, on time. Each time you incur a late charge on a payment because of delay in repaying, it ends up showing as a slow payment on your credit report. You want to avoid those if possible, particularly when you're going to apply for a big mortgage and it's close as it is here."

Charles nodded, then wanted to know what he could do if the credit company made an error.

Alice pointed out that the Federal Trade Commission regulated credit investigating companies. In addition, if a lender turns down a loan based on a credit agency, the lender is required to furnish the applicant with the name and address of the company along with the reason for denial. You can go directly to the credit agency to clarify any inaccuracies.

"The second part of your credit and qualifying statement is your 'net worth'."

NET WORTH

On the net worth sheet, Charles had to list all his assets (net worth is assets minus liabilities). These included the following:

Real estate (location, owned free and clear or mortgaged)

Automobiles (year, make, and model)

Furniture

Clothing

Stocks

Bonds

Cash

Mutual funds

Jewelry

Collectibles

Other

Against these assets, Charles had to indicate the amount of mortgages or loans he had.

Reasons for Giving Net Worth

"Why would you possibly want to know this kind of information?"

"It helps to give us an overall credit picture. We want to be sure that the person we make the mortgage to has a substantial net worth for two reasons:

1. In the event that there should be an interruption of income, as caused by a layoff from work, the person has sufficient assets to rely upon.

2. The borrower isn't someone who has nothing and is therefore going to rush out and buy many more things besides the house in question.

"We assume a certain debt ratio when we make the mortgage. But, if you, for example, don't have a car or furniture or even clothes, once you get the mortgage, you might have to run out and buy all these items. It could adversely affect your debt ratio. But, it would happen *after* we've loaned you the money and be out of our control. On the other hand, if we see on your net worth sheet that you have all these items, then it's far less likely you'll have to go out and buy them. You'll be more likely to maintain a healthy debt ratio."

"Do you mean that if I didn't list a car, it might adversely affect my qualifying?"

"It could. Or if you listed a very old car, which might indicate that you would have to go out and buy a new one soon.

"These two sheets of paper, the credit application and the net worth description help us determine your credit worthiness. They are critical in determining if you get the mortgage."

"So, once you see what I make and my credit history and net worth,you decide to give me the money, right?"

Alice smiled, "Not quite. There are a few more things."

THE MORTGAGE BANKER'S FUNCTION

"You're applying for money through a mortgage banker. In many cases, if we think you qualify, we'll actually fund the money. But, we only put our money up for a short time, perhaps a month or two at the longest. Then, we sell the mortgage to an investor. It could be a savings and loan association, a pension fund, an insurance company, even a wealthy individual, or a secondary lender."

"You mean you're just the broker?"

"Not exactly. We do put up the money at first ourselves, so that's more than a broker.

"Actually, what we do is arrange in advance with lenders to deliver them a certain number of mortgages by a certain time at a certain yield. For example, we promise to deliver 100 mortgages by June 30 at no less than an average yield of 14 percent for a total amount of no less than $5 million.

"Then we go to a bank and arrange a line of credit of, for example, $5 million . Finally, borrowers such as yourself come to us. Using our line of credit, we fund your mortgage. Then, when we have our 100 mortgages, we sell them off to the ultimate lender and pay back our line of credit."

"Sounds complicated."

"It really isn't. But, it's expensive. It usually costs us between 2 and 2½ percent of the loan amount for all the paperwork and the interest on the money we borrow."

"But, I was led to understand that my charge for obtaining this loan," Charles spoke indignantly, "was only going to be 1½ percent. 'One and a half points,' the broker said."

"That's correct. Our cost will be 2½ percent, yours will be 1½. We'll lose 1 percent of the mortgage ($80,000 × 1% = $800) when we make this mortgage for you."

Charles shook his head. He said it didn't make sense.

"We make our money on servicing," Alice said. "We collect the monthly payment from you for ½ percent a year of the mortgage amount. That eventually pays for all our costs and allows us a profit."

"I see," Charles nodded. "But, how does all this affect me?"

"It affects you in several ways. Most important is in the sense that you have to satisfy not only us, but the lender to whom we'll eventually sell your mortgage. That means you can't simply convince me in person. You have to convince the ultimate lender on paper. You've already done that in part with the credit application and the net worth statement. But, there are other forms to fill out."

DOCUMENTS

In addition to the credit terms, Charles was asked to sign an employment verification for his employer. The form asked his employer to verify in writing (by signing a document) Charles' exact salary on either an hourly, weekly, monthly, or annual basis; how long Charles had worked for the company; how much money he had already received in salary thus far that year; and what his chances for continued employment were.

In addition, Charles had to have his bank and any other institution at which he had money sign a similar form stating the amount Charles had on deposit and for how long he had had it.

All of these forms were mailed directly from the mortgage banker to the bank and the employer and then mailed directly back. The idea was that Charles could not intercept them and possibly change the figures or the statements.

In addition, the following documents were also included in the loan "package."

Loan Package Documents

Loan application*

Agreement to costs: A statement that the borrower understands costs involved in the sale and agrees to them

Agreement to not borrow down payment: A statement that the borrower has his or her own cash for the down payment and is not borrowing money for this sum (other than already stated).

Agreement to occupy property for 6 months: A statement that the borrower intends to use the property as a personal residence and willl not rent it out or use it as an investment property for at least 6 months. This is a condition of most home loans today.

Statement of price: Borrower indicates the actual price paid. This is to verify that an inflated price was not used to trick the lender into giving an inflated mortgage amount.

Agreement for impounds: The borrower states whether or not he or she wants the taxes and insurance collected monthly by the lender (impounds). For mortgages over 80 percent of the value of the property, impounds are usually mandatory. For under 80 percent, they are usually optional.

Declaration to lender: A statement that the borrower will occupy the property within 30 days and will not immediately resell to someone else

Statement of finance charges: The borrower indicates that he or

---

* Already discussed

she knows the actual amount of the mortgage payment, and the annual percentage rate (APR).*

These are the documents which Charles had to sign *just for the mortgage banker.* They do not include the documents which the title insurance company required him to sign when he finally made the purchase of the home. In your case, there might be more or fewer documents. But in general, these are the ones that most often show up. Be prepared to sign a great many items.

Also, be prepared to discuss *any* items which you do not understand. If you do not receive an explanation which makes sense to you, *don't sign.* Take the document to a real estate broker or an attorney you can trust and have them explain it. Mortgage bankers and other lenders can make mistakes. You don't want to be one of their mistakes.

Finally, Alice told Charles that there was one more item that was needed, an appraisal of the property.

PROPERTY APPRAISAL

"But," Charles commented, "we already know what the sales price is. Why bother having it appraised now?"

"The reason," Alice said, "is that the lender wants to know that there's real value in the property. For all the lender knows, you and the seller could have gotten together to jack up the price just to get a high loan. To avoid this possibility, we have an independent appraiser go out and check on the property. This will cost you $150 which you'll have to pay whether or not the deal goes through."

Charles sat back abruptly. "Why should I pay even if I don't get the mortgage?"

"Because," Alice said, "we have to pay the appraiser whether or not you buy. You want the mortgage, you have to pay us to have your house appraised."

Charles agreed.

Alice called upon an appraiser, Caroline, who went out to the property. The appraiser measured the house to determine the square

---

* Sometimes the APR will be higher than the mortgage interest rate. Often the reason for this is that the APR will include in it the points paid up front to get the mortgage.

footage. Caroline next checked the condition of the house and the yard noting any additions to the property the former owner had made, as well as any items in poor condition. Finally, Caroline made note of whether the property was on a particularly good lot or an especially bad one.

Then, Caroline went back to her office and, using her books of homes sold in the area, determined what recent sales had been for homes comparable to the one which Charles was buying. She found they were all within the $100,000 to $110,000 price range. Caroline then wrote up her appraisal with comments. The bottom line was that her appraisal of the property was $105,000.

Charles smiled when Alice told him what the appraisal had been. It indicated that he was indeed getting a good price.

"There's only one more document the lender will require prior to closing this deal," Alice said. "It's a termite clearance. In our area, termites are abundant and we have to know the house is clear of them before a mortgage can be funded."

The termite clearance cost $50. The inspector determined there were no termites, but there was a fungus growth in one bathroom, which was cleared up for an additional $60.

When Charles dropped back in to see Alice to find out about the termite report, he asked if that was everything?

She indicated that it just about was. "Of course, there's the actual mortgage papers, which we'll have you sign at the escrow office upon closing. And that will be it."

On the West coast, and for most of the United States, real estate transactions are handled by independent, state-authorized escrow companies. They act as third parties protecting the buyer's funds and the seller's property until the transaction is closed. Many also hold the double function of providing title insurance.

In parts of the East coast, however, an older method is used. Instead of an escrow company, the entire transaction is handled by real estate attorneys, one each for the buyer, seller, and lender. The only real difference between the two methods is that sometimes the attorney fees together come to a bit more than the escrow fee. I have always sought to use the escrow-company method myself

Charles got his mortgage and bought the property. He had handled the entire process himself and was very satisfied in what he had accomplished.

WHY USE A MORTGAGE BANKER?

Charles' experience will soon be repeated by literally millions of buyers across the country. The documents may change name, but essentially, the exchange between borrower and mortgage banker will remain the same.

I chose a mortgage banker for this example for a very specific reason. Prior to 1980, when a person wanted a real estate mortgage, he or she usually dropped into the local savings and loan association. The experience there was considerably different from the one Charles experienced with Alice.

For one thing, most S&Ls had their own mortgage portfolio. Unlike the mortgage banker, they didn't intend to fund the money for a month or two and then sell the mortgage to another lender. They intended to keep the mortgage for its entire life.

Being the ultimate lender, the S&L could be more lenient, if it wanted to, with its qualifying. It could take a closer look at Charles' credit, income-to-debt ratio, and other factors, not the least of which could be the loan officer's personal comments, and then decide whether or not to make a mortgage. A thing as simple as the fact that Charles was a long-time outstanding member of the community in which the S&L had its office might make a difference.

Prior to 1980, more than half of the borrowers who wanted mortgage money went to S&Ls and got what amounted to superior treatment. But, the reason Charles didn't go to a S&L was that in his area at the time, none were making real estate mortgages! The S&Ls were making car loans and consumer loans and some short 3- to 5-year second mortgages. But, they were basically out of the long-term mortgage business, even with SAMs and ARMs.

That's not to say that all savings and loan associations aren't going to handle real estate mortgages in the future. Far from it, they will be an important, perhaps the most significant, aspect of the market. But, they will never again have the prominence they once had.

In today's market, the borrower really needs a mortgage finder. The borrower needs someone who knows who's offering what at the time and at what terms. Since most borrowers are in no way equipped to handle this type of investigation, they go to an expert who is. That expert is the mortgage banker.

The Broker versus the Banker

It is important to understand the difference between a mortgage *broker* and a mortgage *banker,* which is a common misunderstanding.

A mortgage *broker* is usually a real estate broker who, for a fee, will find a lender for a buyer/borrower. The broker collects the fee for putting lender and borrower together with one another. In some cases the broker will also handle the paperwork.

A mortgage *banker* does all of the work of a mortgage broker, but additionally, the banker also often funds the mortgage out of its own personal funds or lines of credit. The mortgage banker is usually the initial lender, as was the case with Charles and Alice in this chapter.

Additionally, the mortgage banker acts as the party which collects the monthly payment, assesses late charges, and handles foreclosures, should they become necessary.

Finally, with the exception of the one to two points collected up front (and which the borrower almost always has to pay regardless of what lender he or she goes to), the mortgage bankers get paid *by the lender.* The mortgage broker usually adds a fee onto the top of the initial points. The mortgage broker usually gets paid by the borrower.

TWELVE

Mortgage Instruments

In the new mortgage game, we banter on about "first," "second," "third," and other mortgages as if we were talking about hamburgers and hot dogs. But, just what are these mortgage instruments that we deal with so lightly? Indeed, what are any of the mortgage devices such as "wraparounds" or "contracts of sale"? The answers are what we'll discover in this chapter.

MORTGAGE VERSUS DEED OF TRUST

Traditionally, in the United States, when a person wanted to borrow money and give real estate as collateral, he or she didn't get a loan. The borrower got a mortgage.

This mortgage differed significantly from other types of loans in that it specifically listed the property as collateral. There were two parties to the mortgage. There was the "mortgagor" who borrowed the money and the "mortgagee" who lent it.

Mortgages were written so that the mortgagor would have a specified amount of time in which to pay back the mortgage and interest on the money. In the event that the mortgagor for any reason was unable to pay back the money, he or she (after missing a payment or two) would be notified that they were in "default." Simply that they were not making the payments.

When a mortgagor was in default, the mortgagee (lender) could then proceed with "foreclosure."

"Foreclosure" was the process whereby the mortgagee would wrest title away from the mortgagor and then sell the property at an open sale to the highest bidder in an attempt to recoup the money originally loaned out plus interest and expenses.

It's important to see here that the borrower or the mortgagor *did not give up title* to the property when he or she applied for a mortgage. Rather, the mortgage papers simply gave the lender or the mortgagee the right to go to court and have the court take away the motgagor's title *if* the payment were not made.

This process of borrowing on property, but not giving up the use of the property is technically called "hypothecation," and it is critical to borrowing on real estate.

Note to reader: This chapter is intended only to give an overview of financing, not to provide legal advice on mortgage instruments. For any legal questions concerning mortgages or what to do in your own particular situation, you should consult with a real estate attorney.

Foreclosure

There is, however, one significant problem with foreclosure—time. If the mortgagor fails to make the payments, the major recourse of the mortgagee (besides assessing late charges *if* called for in the mortgage document), is foreclosure. But, traditionally in order to foreclose on a mortgage, the mortgagee has to go to court. In many cases, the mortgagor was entitled to a court trial and even a jury.

While the law may have been clear and the mortgagee may have won the court test, it took time. Depending on the state, it could have taken anywhere from a few months to a few years. During this period of time, the mortgagee would not have the use of his or her money, nor the use of the property, nor the ability to resell the property.

Of course, it was not all peaches and cream for the mortgagor either. That person might also be expelled from the property pending a court outcome, and might be barred from receiving any rents.

Right of Redemption

All in all, it was a dismal situation. What made it infinitely worse for the mortgagee was something called a "right of redemption." The old theory was that, not only was a home a person's castle, it was something as sacred as the family. Therefore, even *after* a mortgagee had lost property to a mortgagor, even after the mortgagor had gained the right to sell the property to recoup the money borrowed, in many instances the mortgagee retained the right to redeem the property *if* he or she could then come up with the original money borrowed plus interest and costs. The right of redemption in some cases existed for as long as 5 years after the formal foreclosure!

You might imagine the problems this posed for the mortgagee. After getting the property back, the mortgagee would naturally want to resell to get back the borrowed money. But, who would buy knowing that the mortgagor might at sometime in the future suddenly go back to court with sufficient funds to redeem the property? This was particularly a problem when property prices accelerated and the property was worth considerably more after a few years. While the mortgagor might have easily let it go to foreclosure initially, when he or she realized it was now worth 50 percent more and there was that right of redemption in force, why not try to get it back? And the poor person who had been unwise enough to purchase while a right of redemption existed might find that suddenly the property was taken back.

Deficiency Judgment

The redemption period which benefited the mortgagee was offset in part by a benefit which the mortgagee had. When the mortgage was foreclosed through court action and the property sold to pay the loan back plus expenses, there was always the possibility that the property would not yield enough money to cover all the outstanding costs. For example, the mortgage might be for $10,000 plus an additional $1000 in expenses. But when sold, the property might only yield $8000. This would amount to a loss of $3000 for the mortgagee.

However, when the mortgage was foreclosed through court action, the mortgagor might be allowed a "deficiency judgment." This meant that in the event the property did not bring enough money to pay the mortgage, the mortgagee could now go after the mortgagor's other assets. It meant that the mortgagor could be held personally liable for any loss that the mortgagee suffered on the property.

Purchase-Money Mortgages

The idea behind the deficiency judgment was that the mortgagor or borrower might have tricked the mortgagee or lender into loaning more than the property was worth. This protected the lender.

But, there was another side to this. On occasion, unscrupulous sellers would sell a property to a buyer at an unconscionable price, carrying back a big mortgage. The idea was that sooner or later the buyer would discover that he or she had been cheated. At that point, the buyer would stop making payments. The mortgagee would then foreclose. But, what was more important, the mortgagee would resell the property and, since it had originally been way over price, receive far below the mortgage amount. Finally, the mortgagee would get a deficiency judgment against the mortgagor and go after his or her other property.

The whole point of this scam was that the mortgagee, by means of a false sale, could ultimately get the mortgagor's other property (not to mention a down payment and other costs).

To protect buyers from unscrupulous sellers, many states enacted "purchase-money laws." These laws stated that *if the mortgage was part of the* ***purchase*** *price, no deficiency judgment was allowed.* Many states still have this purchase money law in effect.

The purchase-money law is a critical factor of which to be aware when we become involved in financing property. For example, in the chapter on creative financing, we saw how an unscrupulous buyer might get a seller to take back a second mortgage for far more than the house's value while slipping a bigger first underneath. (This came under the heading of cash back to buyer on sale.)

In our example, the poor seller ended up with a $40,000 mortgage with only $20,000 worth of collateral in the house. What can this seller/mortgagee do in the event the buyer/mortgagor allows the property to go into default?

Obviously, he or she can foreclose. But, just as obviously, with the house worth far less than the mortgage amount, the mortgagee isn't going to get his or her money out. The answer is to attempt to get a deficiency judgment through court action.

But, if the state in which this happens has a purchase-money law, no deficiency judgment is possible. Remember, the second mortgage was given as *part of the purchase price* and therefore comes under the law. The poor mortgagee has little recourse. And the sneaky buyer could walk away from the deal no strings attached. (And you thought real estate was all straightforward!)

Purchase money laws are largely unchanged from the early 1930s, when many of them were enacted. But, something else fairly new has come about in real estate financing—something which cured the problem of "time" involved in foreclosure. It was a new mortgage instrument which essentially *eliminated* all of the following:

1. Court foreclosure

2. Redemption

3. Deficiency judgment

The new mortgage instrument which is being used increasingly throughout the United States is the "deed of trust."

DEED OF TRUST

The deed of trust (or trust deed as it sometimes is called) came into existence out of necessity, rather than design. The way I imagine it happening is something like this:

Rachel wanted to borrow money on her property, so she went to her friend Zeke, and asked for $10,000. Zeke had the money and he was willing to lend it. But, he didn't want to get involved with the whole process of mortgage. He liked Rachel and, if she didn't pay back the money, he didn't want to have to take her to court and have a public trial. What's more, if she didn't pay, he wanted to know he would get his money back and quickly.

Zeke thought about it for some time, then finally came up with this idea which he discussed with Rachel.

"I'll lend you the $10,000," he began. "But, I don't want a mortgage on the property. Instead, I want you to issue a deed to me."

"But," Rachel protested, "I don't want to sell. I only want to borrow."

"Yes, I know. I promise that I won't execute the deed (record it, as we'll see shortly) unless you don't make your payments. And when you fully pay off the $10,000, I'll give you your deed back."

Rachel thought about that for awhile, then said, "But, how can I trust you not to take my property? After all, you will have a deed to you from me in your possession."

Now it was Zeke's turn to think. After some pondering, he came up with an extraordinary idea. "Instead of making the deed out to me, you'll make it out to the Parson Dithers. You trust him, don't you?"

Rachel nodded.

"You'll make out the deed to Parson Dithers and include with it instructions that he is to deed the property to me *only* if I inform him and give proof that you're not paying back the money borrowed. He'll hold it in trust for both of us. Since he's an independent third party, it would work fine."

After some consideration, Rachel agreed.

And so the trust deed might have been born.

Of course, court cases and practical application have formalized the procedure. In most cases today, there is a formal instrument, a trust deed which the borrower executes. The borrower is called the "trustor." And the person who performs Parson Dither's job becomes the "trustee." The trustee today is usually an escrow or title insurance company. And today, giving a trust deed does not infringe upon the title of the property, except to the amount of the money borrowed. That means that a borrower/trustor can give a "first" trust deed, "second," a "third," and so on, just as in the case of mortgages.

Finally, the lender under the trust deed system is called the "beneficiary."

Today, trust deeds are used in most places in the United States. In fact, in this book, wherever we've used the term mortgage (for convenience) we might just as well substitute the term "trust deed."

The beauty of a trust deed comes about in the event the trustor does not perform up to the terms of the instrument. At that time, the beneficiary informs the trustee that the trustor (borrower) is in default.

The process of foreclosure in every state is spelled out precisely. For example, in California, after a notice of default is filed, the trustor (borrower) has 90 days in which to make up all back payments, late charges, and lost interest. If the trustor does this, the trust deed is taken out of default and all is as it was before.

If, however, the trustor is not able to do this, after the 90-day waiting period, the trustee begins advertising the property for sale in a legal paper. The advertising continues for 3 weeks. During this time, the trustor may redeem the property only by *paying off* the entire mortgage amount plus any interest and costs.

Finally, after the advertising period, the property is sold "on the courthouse steps" to the highest bidder.

The trustor loses all rights to the property after the sale, including any right of redemption. The beneficiary (lender), however, loses any right to a deficiency judgment.

It works out neatly and cleanly for all concerned. (In California, at the option of the beneficiary, the trustee can go through formal court foreclosure proceedings, although this is rarely done. In that case, redemption and deficiency judgments might be allowed.)

ORDER OF MORTGAGES

We've spent a lot of time talking about firsts, seconds, thirds, and so forth. But exactly what are we talking about here?

It all has to do with the process of "recording." In every county and township across the country there is an official "recorder's office." While there are several different methods of recordation, essentially it is here that the public may "record" important documents.

What does "record" mean?

It means that a notation or a copy of the document along with the legal description of the property is placed into a book that is open to anyone to inspect. Technically, it is called giving "constructive" notice. It's like advertising to the public the title condition of a piece of property.

Normally, once a document has been recorded, it is assumed that everyone knows about it (whether they've seen it or not). The reason is that they have the opportunity, if they desire, to go down to the recorder's office and find the legal description of a piece of property they are concerned about and then check the title. (In some cases, other types of notice such as advertising in a legal paper or taking physical possession may also be necessary, but that's beyond the scope of our discussion here.)

In terms of trust deeds and mortgages, this recording is critical.

When Recording Pays Off

Hal wanted to borrow $50,000 on his property, which was free and clear. He went to ABC Savings and Loan, and they agreed to give him the money in exchange for a trust deed on the property. But, at this point, a certain logistics problem occurred. They would only give him the trust deed if it were a "first." That meant that it was the first trust deed recorded on the property. (As we saw earlier, the chronological order in which the trust deeds or mortgages are placed on the property determines the order of foreclosure. The first gets paid off fully first. Then if there's any money left, the second gets paid off fully. Then, if any money is left, the third, and so on.)

Naturally, holding a first is the best position, and ABC wanted it. But, how could they be sure that Hal hadn't already given someone else a trust deed? If he had, then automatically their trust deed would be a second or lower.

The answer is recording. It's not simply giving the trust deed that counts. It's *recording* it. the trust deed that is *recorded* first becomes the first. That *recorded* second becomes the second, and so forth.

To ensure its position, ABC Savings and Loan searched the title to be sure that Hal hadn't previously recorded any other trust deeds. Satisfied that he hadn't, they agreed to give him the money one morning at 8:00 AM, but not before.

When Hal wanted to know why, they explained what they proposed to do. The recorder's office opened at 8:00 AM. They would be the first there. They would quickly search the title once more to be sure he hadn't placed another trust deed on the books. If he hadn't, they would quickly record theirs and it would immediately take effect. Then, once their position was secure, they would give him the money.

Hal's reply to this was simple, "Why should I trust you? You could record the document and then never give me the money."

ABC saw his point. So they arranged for an independent third party to handle the title search, the recording, and the dispersion of funds. This third party is called an "escrow." In addition, they arranged for title insurance, which guarantees that the escrow company did its work correctly and that the position of the first mortgage was as claimed.

And there you have it. That's how mortgages are recorded and how recordation determines which is first, second, third, and so forth.

More Concerns

Of course, in reality, we've only skimmed the surface. There's much more to this than meets the eye, and I would suggest that anyone involved in a mortgage who is unfamiliar with the trade, consult with a real estate attorney. The attorney might look for some of the following conditions which may or may not be in the trust deed or mortgage:

Due-on clause: We've already indicated that this means the mortgage is due upon sale or transfer of title of the property. While the due-on clause may be unenforceable for many savings and loans and banks and other institutional lenders, it may very well be enforceable if the lender is an individual! Check with your attorney.

Or more: This neat little term when placed after the monthly payment such as "payable at $50 a month or more" indicates that the borrower may pay back any amount of the mortgage at any time *without a penalty*. If you want the mortgage to include a prepayment penalty, you have it written in and the "or more" taken out.

Plus interest or including interest: Here are two cute little terms which can make a big difference. "Plus interest" means that monthly payment may only be a payback of principal, with interest accruing. "Including interest" means the payment may *include* the interest.

In addition, there are other items your attorney will want to watch out for such as a "balloon payment."

Most trust deeds and mortgages which have balloon payments don't mention it. They simply say that the borrower will pay back X amount of dollars per month, "all due and payable in 3 years" (or whatever number of years).

It might read something like this: With a loan amount of $5000, the borrower would agree to repay, "$50 per month including 12 percent per annum interest, all due and payable in 3 years."

Does the above mortgage have balloon payment?

It certainly does! Figure it out for yourself.

$ 50		Monthly payment
× 36		3 years worth of payments
1800	$1800	Maximum amount paid back
5000		Amount borrowed
× 12		Interest rate
600		Interest per year
× 3		Number of years
$1800	– 1800	Total interest
	$ 0	Principal repaid during 3-year period

A mortgage written as above has a balloon payment of $5000 after 3 years! It is essentially an interest-only mortgage. The reason is that the monthly payment is only high enough to pay off the interest. It's not high enough to pay back the principal.

To fully amortize the above mortgage, the monthly payment would have to be $166 per month.

Beware of mortgages with unreasonably low monthly payments. Almost invariably somewhere along the line they contain a big single payment—a "balloon."

YIELD

As we've noted elsewhere, junior mortgages (as seconds, thirds, and so on are sometimes called) are frequently discounted. This means that, when it comes time to sell the mortgage for cash, the lender may not be able to get the face amount. Instead, something less will be obtained.

The reason for this has to do with "yield." The yield on a mortgage is the actual amount of interest it will return. The actual amount is quite often different from the amount stated on the face of the mortgage.

It all has to do with how much money is borrowed and how much is paid back *per year* in interest.

For example, if $10,000 is borrowed at 10 percent interest for 1 year, the yield would be 10 percent. That seems fairly straightforward.

Now, however, let's say that the lender wants to sell this mortgage instrument for cash. There are buyers. But, the buyers want a yield of 20 percent, given the then-current market conditions. How can the lender sell a 10 percent, $10,000 mortgage so that it will yield 20 percent?

The answer is the discount. Forgetting about amortization for a moment, we'll assume that this mortgage pays back exactly $1000 in interest over the year.

$10,000	Mortgage amount
× .10	Interest rate
$ 1,000	Interest returned

No matter what, the total amount of interest returned on this mortgage in terms of cash is not going to be more than $1000. Yet, the person willing to buy the mortgage will buy it only if the true yield (or true interest) is 20 percent. How much does the $10,000 mortgage have to be discounted to yield a 20 percent return?

$1000	Actual cash returned
÷ .20	Yield desired
$5000	Discount

The answer is that the mortgage has to be discounted by $5000! This only makes sense. If someone lends out $5000 at 20 percent interest, they will indeed get back $1000 in interest over one year.

$5000	Mortgage amount
× .20	Interest rate
$1000	Interest returned

Of course, we also have to take into account term. In our mortgage of $10,000 at 10 percent, if it's for 2 years, the return would be $1000 short per year or $2000. To get a 20 percent yield our actual discount, therefore, would be 20 percent.

Buyers of mortgages whether they be firsts, seconds, or whatever, only speak in terms of yield. The yield they desire determines the discount they demand.

One other aspect of yield which needs to be mentioned is time. In the mortgage above, we only considered a term of 2 years. But, in actual practice, most mortgages, even seconds are for from 3 to 5 years.

For the cash buyer of such a mortgage, this means that his or her money is going to be tied up for a considerable period of time. During that time, a new round of inflation could set in and interest rates could shoot up. Interest rates going higher than the yield received on the second could mean an ultimate loss for this cash buyer. So most buyers of seconds will add into their price a further factor in yield for time. If our cash buyer were willing to accept a 20 percent yield on a 1-year mortgage, he or she might demand 22 percent for a 3-year mortgage or even 24 for a 5-year term.

Of course, it should be understood that these yield demands are not entirely arbitrary. They are based on the competitive cost of borrowing money in the short-term market.

It also should be understood that they work the other way as well. If you have a $10,000 second mortgage on which you are being paid 20 percent interest for 1 year and, at the time, 10 percent is considered a good yield, you might very well be able to sell the mortgage for considerably more in cash!

(If this seems all vaguely familiar to you, perhaps it's because you've been involved in the bond market. It works in a similar fashion.)

WRAPAROUNDS

Another type of very old mortgage which has come back into favor recently is the "wraparound," technically called an "all-inclusive mortgage" (AIM) or an "all-inclusive trust deed" (AITD).

The wrap was once popular for certain tax advantages it offered. These advantages are today largely gone. But, it has gained new favor for two reasons:

1. It can increase the yield to the seller on the sale of a piece of property.
2. It can give the seller increased safety.

Of course, there are many dangers inherent in the wrap, and the best advice is not to get involved in one unless you first have it checked out with a competent real estate attorney.

In general, a wraparound is much like a second mortgage, with a couple of important differences. It always involves at least one mortgage, a first usually existing on the property and perhaps one or more junior mortgages. It works like this.

Sidney has an existing 10 percent mortgage for $50,000 on her property. She is willing to carry back another $50,000 in paper to help the buyer make the purchase. (She expects the buyer to put $20,000 in cash down.) Sidney, however, instead of asking for a $50,000 second, wants a $100,000 wrap.

Our buyer is Harold. He has the down payment and he wants to buy. Only he doesn't understand what Sidney means by a wrap. She explains it to him in this fashion:

"Instead of your *assuming* my original first mortgage, and my giving you a second mortgage, you'll just buy my property *subject to* (which means you're aware of the first but not assuming payment for it) and will give me a $100,000 wrap."

Harold still looked puzzled, so Sidney continued, "You'll only have *one mortgage* for $100,000. That's it. You'll pay me on it. And it will be a great advantage to you. Current interest rates are 15 percent, but I'll give you this wrap for only 14 percent. You'll save a whole interest point."

"But," Harold objected, "what about the first mortgage?"

"It's mine," Sidney said. "I took it out and I'll keep it. From the money you pay me, I'll make the payments on it. You won't have to worry about it."

"But, what if you don't make the payments on it and the first forecloses?"

Sidney thought about that. "We'll write into the wrap that if I don't continue making the payments on the first, you have the right to assume it and make the payments and subtract them from the amount you pay me."

Harold thought it over. It seemed fair and he would be getting 1 percent lower interest than the market rate. It was a good deal, he thought.

Yield

Indeed, it probably was a good deal, although he might have wanted to look out for some problems we'll consider in a moment. But for now, let's look at the deal from Sidney's viewpoint.

Sidney is giving a $100,000 mortgage at 14 percent interest. Forgetting about amortization for the moment, that means that she will receive about $14,000 in interest the first year

$100,000	Mortgage amount
× 14%	Interest rate
$ 14,000	Interest paid first year

From this amount, she will now have to make a payment on the existing first mortgage. That first, however, is at 10 percent.

$50,000	Existing first
× 10%	Interest rate
$ 5,000	Approximate first-year interest

$ 14,000	Interest received from Harold
− 5,000	Interest paid on first
$ 9,000	Additional interest received by Sidney

Because she only has to pay 10 percent on the first, her interest charges there are only $5000. But, she receives back $14,000 from Harold, giving her a net interest of $9000. Now, what is her true yield?

Remember, Sidney only advanced $50,000. (The other $50,000 was the existing first mortgage.)

$ 9,000	Net interest
÷ 50,000	Existing first
.18	Yield

Sidney's true yield on the $50,000 mortgage amount she advanced (her equity in the property, which she loaned to Harold) actually came to 18 percent.

What Sidney has done, in effect, is to gain the benefit of the low-interest first mortgage. If Harold had been smart, he might have said to Sidney, "I won't give you a wrap. I'll give you a second mortgage at 16 percent and I'll assume the first." He would still have been better off. *He* would have gotten the benefit of the low-interest first.

But, by using the wrap, all the benefits went to Sidney and she managed to get the equivalent of an 18 percent yield on the money she actually loaned out.

Of course, Harold wasn't weeping. For him, there was still a single mortgage at 1 percent below market interest rates. Besides, he didn't have any idea of what he had lost out on.

Safety

Sidney had one additional reason for desiring the wrap—safety.

She really didn't trust Harold. She didn't know if he would continue making payments on the first if he assumed it. If she had given a simple second mortgage and Harold had assumed the first and then not paid, she might not have known about it for several months. Typically, institutional lenders allow their borrowers 2 to 5 months to get behind before they will actually institute foreclosure.

If the first foreclosed, Sidney, in order to protect her interests under a second, would have to then foreclose and make good all the payments on the first, including up to 5 months interest and costs.

However, because *she* was making the payment directly to the first under the wrap, she would know exactly when Harold stopped making payments, if he did. She would have far greater control. She would keep the first out of foreclosure.

(It's been my experience that some investors in real estate very quickly pick up on the concept of a wrap, while others have great difficulty with it through no fault of their own. If you're in the latter group, my suggestion is that you simply stay away from wraparounds.)

There are a few dangers inherent in the wrap of which Harold or Sidney or both may not have been aware. Some first mortgages, particularly those which may have been sold to a government secondary lender, prohibit wraps. For example, if the first was through a federal savings and loan association which had a due-on clause which was enforceable, that lender might immediately institute foreclosure proceedings as soon as it found out the property was sold.

Sidney might have set up the deal, Harold accepted, they both gone forward, only to find *after* the deal was closed that suddenly the first mortgage demanded immediate full payment. That could be a disaster for all concerned. It's another good reason to be sure you consult with a good attorney before getting involved in a wrap.

One last consideration is the language of the wrap. In most states, there is no formalized wraparound in the same way that there is a formalized mortgage or trust deed. Rather, it is drawn up case by case.

If your broker or seller (or buyer) draws one up well, there could be no problems. But, however, if it is drawn up badly, all sorts of trouble could ensue. Again, a competent attorney is the answer.

I don't mean to be scaring you away from wraps. They do have enormous advantages, both to the buyer and the seller. But, you should be aware that they, like other mortgage instruments, do have some drawbacks and pitfalls.

CONTRACT FOR SALE

The "contract for sale" (sometimes also called the "contract for deed") is the last mortgage instrument we'll consider. It has been around as long as the mortgage itself, perhaps longer. In recent years, however, it has come into favor once again as a means of defeating the due-on clause in fixed interest-rate mortgages.

Contract for sale in its operation is the essence of simplicity. A seller simply says to a buyer, "I will keep the title to the property until you can pay me for it. Then when you pay me, I will issue you a deed. In the meantime, we'll have a contract for that deed between us."

And that, basically, is all that there is. It's a contract to buy a piece of property. The actual title does not normally change hands.

In the past, the contract of sale was used primarily for buyers who didn't have enough money for a down payment. This occurred most frequently in the purchase of bare land. Hence, the name was originally "the land contract of sale."

Regan wanted to buy Sheila's lot. Sheila wanted $5000 full price. She was willing to give a mortgage for $3000, but she insisted on $2000 cash.

Regan only had $500. So to make the deal, they worked out a contract. Regan would pay Sheila the $500 immediately. Then he would pay her $100 per month until he had paid for 15 months. That would give him the necessary $2000 down. At that time, Sheila would transfer title to him and retain a mortgage for $3000.

$ 500		Initial down payment
1500		In 15 monthly payments of $100
$2000	$2000	Full down payment
	+ 3000	First mortgage
	$5000	Full purchase price

The contract of sale was essentially a way for the borrower to tie up the property until he or she had enough money for a down payment. For the seller it was essentially a way of tying up a borrower. It worked to the advantage of both.

In recent years, the contract of sale evolved into a new application. This came about from the fact that no title changed *until* the full down payment was paid.

Sheila had another piece of property she wanted to sell. It was a house and she had a $50,000 first mortgage on it. She wanted $20,000 down and was willing to give up a $50,000 second.

$ 50,000	First
50,000	Second
20,000	Cash down
$120,000	Full price

It seemed like a straightforward deal. However, there was a hitch. The lender on the first had a due-on clause in the mortgage and refused to allow any assumption. The lender said that if Sheila sold, the mortgage would have to be paid.

Sheila set to work thinking and came up with the idea of a contract of sale. Under a contract, *no title changed hands.* Therefore, the first mortgage lender couldn't insist (she thought) on acceleration (paying off the mortgage).

So Sheila sold her property that way to Sam.

$ 20,000	Cash down
100,000	Contract for sale for five years at 12 percent interest
$120,000	

It worked beautifully. Sam paid Sheila 12 percent on the full $100,000. Sheila then took out enough money to pay the first mortgage (never informing the lender of what she was doing) and kept the rest for herself. In effect, she had the same arrangment as a wraparound. The only difference was that, in addition, she also kept title to the property.

It did work out beautifully, until the lender discovered what was happening. Immediately, the lender began foreclosure proceedings. The lender claimed Sheila's actions constituted a sham sale.

It went to court and in a landmark decision in Lassen County, California in 1976, the court held in favor of Sheila! Subsequent court actions in California (principally the Wallen Kemp decision) not only upheld the case, but broadened the impact so it wasn't even necessary to use a contract-of-sale device.

Nevertheless, in states in which the due-on clause is still in force, some investors and brokers are endeavoring to use the contract of sale to defeat it.*

---

* Entering into a contract of sale for any reason and in particular to defeat a due-on clause is hazardous at best and should only be done upon the advice of an attorney.

For the seller, there are many advantages to the contract of sale, of which we have seen several. For the buyer, the principal advantage is obtaining a home with a smaller down payment or with a lower interest-rate mortgage, or both. For the buyer, however, there also can be a big disadvantage.

When a buyer purchases a home under the more traditional method of transferring title and obtaining a mortgage (or trust deed), he or she has a big benefit, namely the property is in his or her name.

This enables the buyer to refinance, to lease, even to sell.

With a contract of sale, however, the title resides with the seller. This can be a big disadvantage. It may be impossible to refinance, to lease, or to sell.

Additionally, if the seller happens to be unscrupulous, he or she could refinance the property and keep the proceeds. In theory, the seller could even sell the property to someone else! Or, what is more likely, refuse to transfer title to the original buyer even after all the agreed-upon payments had been made.

The reason is the title. In a contract of sale, the buyer only has that—a contract. It may indeed be a legal and binding contract (if properly drawn), but to be enforced, the parties have to go to court in a civil action. That takes time and money. And it puts the buyer in an unreasonably risky position.

To aid buyers, many states have allowed the buyer to record a contract of sale. This, in effect, gives constructive notice that a buyer has an interest in the property and prevents the seller from easily reselling or refinancing.

Nevertheless, a contract of sale remains a tricky financial instrument. Properly used, it can work wonders. But, in the hands of someone inexperienced or ill advised, it can create unbelievable problems.

In the new mortgage game, we would expect to find new mortgage instruments. That's not really the case. The SAMs and ARMs and all the rest use different language, but essentially, they use the old tried and true instruments. The big changes, as we've seen, have been more in their application than in their design.

THIRTEEN

The Tax Implications of Mortgages

If you were to ask the average buyer of real estate what the tax implications of mortgages were, you'd probably get an answer such as, "There aren't any!" Most people don't see any tax consequences of mortgages. After all, when we mortgage our property, we don't report the mortgage to the Internal Revenue Service (IRS). When we receive the money from a mortgage, we don't normally report it as profit. Therefore, general wisdom might ask, where are the tax implications?

Actually, there are many tax implications of mortgages, and even the person who is only buying a residence to live in should be aware of them. Knowing the tax consequences can make the purchase of a home easier or more difficult. In some cases, the tax advantage can make ownership a real possibility where it didn't exist before.

INTEREST DEDUCTION

The first tax consequence of a mortgage is the fact that interest on the mortgage is deductible.

Almost everyone knows this. There is even a place on IRS form 1040, Schedule A which specifically lists "Home Mortgage."* At the end of the year, a mortgage company normally sends the borrower a

* In certain cases, for individuals with high incomes, interest deducted might be taxable under the heading of "minimum tax"—check with your tax accountant or attorney.

note indicating the total interest paid along with total taxes paid. Those two figures, then, can be deducted from the borrower's regular income. In this sense, the mortgage forms a tax shelter.

Using the Interest Deduction to Help Purchase a Home

While it's all well and good to know that at the end of the year the mortgage company will inform us of how much interest we've paid and then we can automatically deduct that from our income taxes, there is another way to handle this interest deduction. It is possible to use it to have the government subsidize our purchase of a home.

Marc has found a house he wants to buy. The purchase price is $120,000. He plans to put $20,000 down and obtain a new first mortgage for $100,000. The new mortgage will be at 14 percent interest. The payments will be $1184 a month.

Although Marc's income is sufficient to allow him to qualify for the mortgage, he is wary of the payment. He feels that all he can really afford is about $1000 a month. This payment is almost $200 more than he really wants to spend. Marc was ready to give up on the purchase until his agent, David, pointed out that the government would in part be subsidizing the purchase.

David pointed out that Marc could deduct the interest on the mortgage from his taxes. That would result in a dollars-and-cents tax savings. David quickly figured it out.

$100,000	Mortgage amount
× 14%	Interest rate
$ 14,000	Approximate first-year interest

David pointed out that Marc would be paying approximately $14,000 in interest the first year (actually somewhat less since the principal balance on which interest is calculated is reduced each month).

"That's a $14,000 deduction off your income taxes. Now, let's see what it's actually worth in dollars and cents saved. What income bracket are you in?"

Marc didn't know the answer to that for sure but guessed that he was probably in the 25 to 35 percent range.

"We'll make a guess that you're in the 30 percent bracket. That means that 30 cents out of the last dollar you make goes to the government in taxes. Now we can figure your tax savings."

$14,000	Interest
× 30%	Tax bracket
$ 4,200	Approximate tax savings

"Of course, you'll want your accountant to check it out, to give you exact figures, since such a big deduction will drop you into a lower tax bracket."

Marc looked at the figure closely. "You mean that my tax bill will be reduced by $4000? I'll have to pay the government $4000 less?"

"Could be," David nodded. "Now, let's see what that works out to monthly.

$4200	Tax savings
÷ 12	Monthly
350	Monthly savings

"Calculated on a monthly basis, the interest you will have to pay will save you as much as $350 a month. If we now subtract that $350 per month from your payments, we come up with a startling figure.

$1184	Principal and interest payment
− 350	Tax savings
$ 834	Actual monthly payment

"Your actual monthly payment isn't $1184. It's only $834, actually far below what you considered to be your maximum amount."

Marc took one look at the calculations and said, "Where do I sign?"

Interest Deductions Come Once a Year, Mortgage Payments Every Month

David beamed, then added. "Of course, while it looks great on paper, you must remember the cash-flow features of this."

Marc looked puzzled, so David explained. "While it may be true that your effective payment will be only $834 a month (less if you're in a higher bracket, more if you're in a lower one), you nevertheless will be committed each month to the full $1184 mortgage payment.

Each month, you will have to come up with the full payment while, chances are, you won't get your tax savings until the end of the year."

Marc shook his head. He still didn't understand.

"Unless you take extra deductions or in some other way reduce your income tax payments, you won't get the benefits of this on a monthly basis. You'll get it one time, at the end of the tax year when you get your tax refund. Yet, you will be making your mortgage payments monthly. If you have enough cash on hand to handle the monthly payment through the year and then get it back after taxes, fine. But, if you're counting on your monthly payment only being $834 a month, and that being the only amount you would have to come up with, you could be in trouble."

Marc nodded. He understood. But the advantages tax-wise were still so great that he wanted to buy.

FINANCING AND TAX "BASIS"

While many people are familiar with the material just covered—the interest deduction against income taxes—few are familiar with another aspect of financing, and that's how it relates to "basis."

This is the sort of thing that most people never think of until it's time to sell—then they get a tax shock that blows them right out of the water. Understanding basis and mortgages can mean thousands, tens of thousands of dollars of difference to all property owners from those who sell their house to those who sell regional shopping centers.

(Note: this material is intended only as an overview. See your own attorney for specific tax questions.)

Real estate, whether it be for investment or for residence purposes, is an asset. It is a capital investment. As such, if we make a gain on it when we sell, there are taxes to pay on that gain. (Of course, with a house we can often roll over that gain by buying another home and meeting certain other conditions.)

The question is, how do we calculate the *gain* on the sale of real estate?

The way most people do it is wrong.

Jason bought a home for $50,000 back in 1975. In 1978, with prices shooting upward, he got a new first mortgage for $65,000. In 1981, he sold the property for $110,000. What was his gain?

Jason thought he knew how to figure it easily.

$110,000	Sales price
− 10,000	Sales costs
$100,000	Net sales price
− 65,000	Mortgage existing
$ 35,000	Gain

According to Jason, he just subtracted the mortgage from the sales price and that was his gain.

Was he right?

Unfortunately, he wasn't. What Jason didn't realize was that, for tax purposes, mortgages *do not count* (except in an installment or deferred-payment sale, which we'll consider in a few moments).

Jason came up with a gain of only $35,000. But, his accountant came up with a gain of $43,000—$8000 higher. Let's see how it was calculated.

How to Calculate the Gain on the Sale

A. In calculating the gain on the sale of an asset, it is necessary to first arrive at its basis. The "basis" simply means the amount on which the gain may be based. It is usually the original purchase price (though not always, as in the case of new construction) plus certain items such as the cost of purchase, minus other items.

B. Once all the items to be added or subtracted (see your accountant) from the price have been determined, we arrive at the original basis. This is the figure from which all future calculations will be made.

C. There are certain items which raise the basis. Capital improvements to the property, such as adding a swimming pool or, in this case, another room, add to the basis. In the case of investment property, depreciation would lower the basis. This calculation is made at the time of sale and gives us our "adjusted basis."

D. Now we must determine what we've sold the property for. The first figure is usually the gross sales price.

E. From the gross sales price we have to subtract costs of sale, which may include escrow and title-insurance charges, real estate commission, recording fees and so forth.

F. Once we subtract the cost, we arrive at the net sales, or the "adjusted" sales, price.

G. Gain is finally determined by subtracting the adjusted basis, which we've already calculated, from the adjusted sales price.
"Gain" is the amount of money on which we will have to pay tax (it's not the tax itself).

Here's how Jason should have figured his gain on the sale of his property.

$ 50,000		Original purchase price	
+ 2,000		Costs of purchase	**A**
52,000		Original basis	**B**
+ 5,000		Extra room added	**C**
57,000		Adjusted basis	
$110,000		Sales price	**D**
− 10,000		Costs of sale	**E**
$100,000		Adjusted sales price	**F**
	$100,000	Adjusted sales price	
	− 57,000	Adjusted basis	
	$ 43,000	Gain on sale	**G**

The important thing for our purposes is to see that the mortgage at no time entered into the calculation of gain. For tax purposes, the property was treated as if he had paid cash.

But, the mortgage did indeed enter into the calculation which Jason originally made. You'll recall that he had an existing mortgage of $65,000 when he sold. It was by subtracting that mortgage from the net sales price that he came up with what he considered gain.

Jason was outraged by his accountant's figures. "After I pay closing costs and subtract the mortgage amount, I only end up with $35,000. Yet, the government says my actual gain is $43,000. It just isn't fair."

His accountant's name was Dove. She smiled gently and said, "Yes, it is fair. Let me show you."

Jason's property

$50,000	Original purchase price
− 10,000	Down payment
$40,000	Original mortgage

"You put $10,000 down when you bought your house and you had a mortgage of $40,000. Then, later, you refinanced and got a new mortgage of $65,000.

$65,000	New mortgage
40,000	Old mortgage paid off
$25,000	Cash to Jason

"You received $25,000 in cash when you refinanced."

"But," Jason countered, "that was 3 years earlier. Besides, the government can't tax me for money I borrow. I got a mortgage for $65,000 in order to get that $25,000 in cash."

"True, you don't pay taxes on money you borrowed. But, when you sold your house, your liability under that mortgage was relieved. Suddenly, it was no longer borrowed money. It became income and contributed to your gain. Here's how your cash flow on your property actually looked:

− $10,000	Down payment when purchased
− 2,000	Closing costs
− 12,000	Put into property at purchase
+ 25,000	From refinance
+ 13,000	Balance after refinance
− 5,000	Cost of room added
8,000	Balance after room addition
+ 35,000	From sale
$43,000	Cash profit to Jason

"You see, if we follow it all the way through on the basis of your cash flow in the property, you actually did make a $43,000 profit."

REFINANCING CAN CAUSE TAX PROBLEMS

"The problem was that because you refinanced, it didn't look as if the profit were actually there. It appeared as if the government was taking more gain than actually existed."

Jason's confusion is perhaps the single most common error made with regard to mortgages and taxes. It is made constantly by sellers. Usually, they make it before they put their home up for sale. Then, after it's sold and they have their accountant calculate their taxes, it hits them like a sledgehammer.

The solution, of course, is to consult with your accountant *before* you put your property up for sale!

(It should be noted that there is a rollover provision in the tax law which provides that, once every 24 months, an owner of a principal residence may defer the payment of taxes on any gain on sale of the principal residence providing it is replaced by a residence of greater value and other specfic conditions are met. Check into Irwin and Brickman, *The Real Estate Agent's and Investor's Tax Book*, McGraw-Hill, for more information here.)

DEFERRING TAXES THROUGH MORTGAGES

Besides the interest paid on a mortgage being deductible, it is possible to defer the payment of taxes on the gain on the sale of property. This is the process of moving the taxes to be paid into the future. The principal method of doing this is the "installment sale."

The rules for the installment sale can be fairly complex, and you should check with an attorney before entering into one, but at their most basic they say, in part, "If the payment for property is received in more than 1 year, then the taxes on the gain may be paid as the payments are made."

Jerry sold his house for $100,000. His gain on the sale was $50,000. Normally, he would pay taxes on that gain in the year of the sale (probably he would pay capital gains taxes, if he and the property qualified).

But, if instead of receiving the entire $50,000 in gain in 1 year, he took it in the form of a mortgage on which he received payment over, for example, 5 years, then his gain would be spread out over 5 years. If he received $10,000 a year for 5 years, instead of paying on a gain of $50,000 in 1 year, he'd pay on a gain of $10,000 a year for each of 5 years.

What's the advantage here?

The advantage is that, as we receive greater amounts of income, we are pushed into higher tax brackets. It stands to reason that we'll be in a lower tax bracket (and thus pay less tax) on $10,000, than on $50,000. By spreading the gain out over 5 years, we may have significantly reduced our actual taxes.

This process has been pushed to the limit by some investors. Some will take payment for 10 years or even 30 years, and $50,000 over 30 years is only $1667 per year on which to pay taxes. Other investors will take one payment in the year of sale and then *no* payments for 10 years. During that time, the borrower (the new buyer) continues to pay them interest on the money, but no principal. Since the seller is only liable for gain (principal), no taxes are paid for 10 years. (Although the interest paid on the money received is of course taxed. See below.)

DEFERRED TAX MORTGAGES CAN BE MORE HEADACHE THAN THEY'RE WORTH

The above procedure does not avoid taxes. It simply moves them into the future. It is also of doubtful value in extreme cases.

Jerry's original deal didn't go through, so he decided to go for an installment sale. He decided to give his prospective buyer a mortgage for $40,000 for 10 years, interest only. The buyer put $10,000 down in cash.

Jerry was liable for taxes paid on the $10,000 down payment as gain in the year of sale. But, for the balance of $40,000, he had no capital gains taxes to pay until year ten, when he actually received the principal. During that time, his borrower only paid him interest.

Jerry thought he had done well, since he got away without paying taxes for so long.

But, did he?

If he had received his capital back, it would probably have been taxed at the capital gains rate. As of this writing, that would be calculated in the following fashion:

Jerry would take 60 percent of this total gain and exclude it. (No taxes would have to be paid on it.) The remaining 40 percent he would then add to his regular income and pay taxes. If he received $10,000 per year in principal return, $6000 would be excluded, and only $4000 added to his regular taxes.

$10,000	Gain
− 6,000	Excluded
$ 4,000	Taxable gain

If he were in a 35 percent tax bracket, his total would be:

$4000	Taxable gain
× 35%	Tax bracket
$1400	Tax to be paid

This would leave Jerry with $8600 to reinvest in real estate or elsewhere (not to mention the interest due on the unpaid balance).

On the other hand, Jerry had elected to receive no principal. Instead, he received the interest on $40,000 annually. This interest was at 14 pecent and came to $5600.

$40,000	Gain not received
× 14%	Interest rate
$ 5,600	Interest on money

Since there was no capital gains advantage on interest, Jerry would have to add the entire $5600 to his regular income and pay taxes on it. His taxes would thus be:

$5600	Interest only on mortgage
× 35%	Tax bracket
$1960	Taxes to be paid

Of course, it could be argued that, while he paid more taxes the second way, he was still maintaining his capital intact. But, in the future, as capital gains taxes become reduced even more than they are at this writing, this procedure will become less and less advantageous. The big problem I see with it is that it ties up the investor's capital in paper, which as we've seen in various chapters, is a lot harder to spend than cash.

We've covered several methods by which taxes can be saved through the use of mortgages. And we've seen how not properly calculating the basis on a piece of property and how incorrectly using a mortgage to calculate profit can lead to some headaches on sale.

There are many other ways in which taxes and mortgages come

together to provide problems as well as advantages for the property owner/taxpayer. These include, among others, tax-deferred exchanges and syndication. For those interested in pursuing this in more detail, I again recommend *The Real Estate Agent's and Investor's Tax Book*, by Irwin and Brickman, McGraw-Hill, 1981.

FOURTEEN

Putting the New Mortgage Game to Work for You

As we've seen, real estate financing is far from dead. And financing, since it is the life blood of real estate itself, means that the housing and the investment market are also very much alive.

But, they are different, almost totally different, from the way they were only a few short years ago. Today, if you don't know an ARM from a SAM you could be in trouble. If you don't understand creative financing, you might not be able to buy the home you want. Today, the rules of the mortgage game have changed. And if you don't know those new rules, you'd better reread this book.

I've saved for this last chapter something which I had originally wanted to put into the introduction. But I later saw it could only be fully explained after reading about the mortgage game. This is the best example of which I know to illustrate the change that's occurred in real estate entirely because of the new financing. And it also illustrates the advantages to both buyer and seller of knowing the new rules. I call it the "two-tier market."

THE TWO-TIER MARKET

In the not-so-distant past, when a house went up for sale, the price that was posted was the one and single price that the seller wanted. It was the price at which the house was offered for sale.

For buyers, it was straightforward. They checked out houses in the multiple listing books of their agents and found the price range they could afford.

For sellers, it was equally straightforward. They found out what comparable houses were selling for in their neighborhood. Then, based on these comparables, they put a price on their house.

That's all changed. Every house on the market now has *two* prices. One price is the *cash price.* The other is the *paper, or financed, price.*

Between these two prices is usually a spread of anywhere from 5 to 30 percent. And that means something incredibly significant to those involved in the sale. For the buyer who understands how the two-tier system works and knows how to use it, it means the possibility of an enormous savings. For the seller who knows how to use it, it can mean the difference between getting "top dollar" or "bottom dollar" on a sale.

We've touched on the concept of the two-tier market in several chapters when we discussed discounting mortgages. But, we've never really applied it specifically to housing prices before. It's when we apply discounting to housing prices that we arrive at the two-tier market.

What the Two-Tier Market Is

Cash price means that the seller gets all cash upon the sale. The seller takes back no part of the financing. This, however, doesn't mean that the property isn't financed. The buyer could have a first, second, third, and so forth. It only means that the financing is handled by the buyer through a lender *other* than the seller.

Paper price means that the seller carries some or all of the financing. In this case, the seller may carry back a second, a first, or a third, or whatever. The more financing the seller carries, the greater the difference between the cash price and the paper price.

Determining the Two Prices of Every Home

How does a person, buyer or seller, know what the cash price and the paper price for a home are? Which of these two corresponds to the old days when there was only one price?

Perhaps the answer to this can be most clearly seen if we take an example.

Harriet wanted to buy Henry's house. Henry had put his house up for sale for $100,000. He wanted the $100,000 in cash. He felt his price was justified. He had checked other recent sales in his area, and houses like his were selling for about $100,000. He felt sure he could sell, too.

Harriet carefully looked over the house and decided she liked it. But, she certainly couldn't pay Harry all cash. She had to have financing.

So Harriet checked out the various ARM and SAM and other mortgages that she might get from a lender. She had $10,000 to put down and discovered that she couldn't qualify for the $90,000 loan she needed. The highest mortgage she could qualify for was $80,000. She was $10,000 short.

So Harriet's broker, Andy, suggested that Harriet offer $90,000. "I'll try to convince Henry to accept it," Andy said.

Harriet made this offer:

$10,000	Cash down
+ 80,000	First mortgage arranged by Harriet
$ 90,000	Cash to seller

Andy presented the offer to Henry. When Henry saw the price, he rejected it out of hand. "I want $100,000. Other houses in this area have been selling for $100,000 and there's no reason I should take less and there's nothing you can say that will make me change my mind."

Andy had been in business for some time and he liked a challenge, so he set out to prove that Henry should accept Harriet's offer.

Comparing Recent Sales

He first pointed out that he had a list of all the sales of homes in Henry's area for the past 6 months. There had been three sales. Indeed, all had been for around $100,000.

SALE	*PRICE, $*
A	106,000
B	96,000
C	99,000

"On the surface, I can see why you would think that your house is worth $100,000, given these sales figures," Andy began.

"What do you mean on the surface?"

"Well," Andy continued, "I've dug a little deeper in the sales. In each of those three sales, I've looked up the financing. Here's what it looks like:

Comparing Financing on Recent Sales

SALE	*FINANCING, $*
A	80,000 (1st carried by seller)
B	20,000 (2d carried by seller)
C	30,000 (2d carried by seller)

"You see, in each of those recent sales, the seller carried back a part of the sales price in the form of a mortgage."

"I don't think you understand," Andy persisted. "They didn't want to carry paper any more than you do. They carried paper because it was the only way they could make the sale. We're living in an age when financing is difficult to come by. They couldn't find any buyers who could qualify for an institutional mortgage, the way Harriet can. So just to sell they had to take paper."

"So you're saying that because Harriet's offering cash, I should lower my price."

"Exactly, cash is worth more than paper."

"What makes you think so?" Henry appeared mildly interested in what Andy was now saying.

"We can actually calculate the 'present value' of paper. That means how much those mortgages are actually worth if they are immediately translated into cash. It has something to do with yield (see Chapter 12) and I won't bother you with the details, except to say that in the cases of 'A,' 'B,' and 'C' the interest rate was far below the current market rate. The sellers had to accept a low rate in order to convince the buyers to go through with the deal. So when it came time to sell the paper for cash, in 'B' and 'C' the discount was 30 percent of the face value of the second mortgage. In 'A,' largely because it was a first, the discount was only 20 percent. It looked like this:

Finding the True Cash Price of Every House Sold

Sale	*Financing, $*	*Discount, %*	*Cash Value, $*	*Cash Lost, $*
A	80,000 (1st carried by seller)	20	65,000	16,000
B	20,000 (2d carried by seller)	30	15,000	6,000
C	30,000 (2d carried by seller)	30	21,000	9,000

"Now when we subtract the money lost by converting the paper into cash, we come up with the real price of the homes sold."

	A	*B*	*C*
Sales price	$106,000	$ 96,000	$ 99,000
Cash lost through discount	16,000	6,000	9,000
True "cash" sales price	$ 90,000	$ 90,000	$ 90,000

Henry looked over the figures, then looked at them again.

"Of course," Andy pointed out, "it doesn't usually work out quite so neatly as this, but I think you get the picture. In terms of *cash,* all three houses in your area sold for exactly $90,000. That means that the offer of Harriet's is perfectly in line."

"But," stammered Henry, "I can get more if I am willing to accept paper."

"Yes, if you're willing to accept about a $33,000 second mortgage, you should be able to obtain your price. You'll get $10,000 more than on a cash deal. Of course, if you were to accept cash, you could take $23,000 in cash and buy a discounted second mortgage worth about $33,000. You see, it all comes out the same way. Your house is worth exactly $90,000 in cash. The price goes up depending on how much financing you are willing to carry. But, the cash price remains the same."

Since Henry wanted cash, he signed.

MOST BUYERS AND SELLERS ARE UNAWARE OF THE TWO-TIER MARKET

Andy was a pretty good agent, and we as buyers and sellers can learn a great deal more from what he said than just his figures conveyed. For in the market place, most sellers are indeed like Henry. They are unaware of the two-tier market. And most buyers, like Harriet, are equally unaware of it.

This provides for certain opportunities, if we can learn to handle the new rules of the mortgage game. For example, as a buyer, we can look for a seller who is willing to sell for the lower *cash* price, yet is also willing to help with the financing. In this manner, we can obtain a bargain.

Or, using a different ploy, as a buyer we can first go out and arrange for our own financing. We can contact a mortgage banker or other lender source and find out exactly what type of financing we can qualify for—the maximum monthly payment, the interest rate, and, most important, the maximum amount. Once we know how much we can borrow, we can approach sellers as *cash* buyers.

For example, if we have $10,000 to put down and we know we can get a $90,000 mortgage, we can come into a seller who is, for example, asking $120,000, and offer $100,000 in cash. If the $120,000 was the paper price, the seller might seriously consider our offer (particularly if it's a tight market). Of course, we would want to be sure we wrote our deal so that it was contingent upon our actually succeeding in getting our financing.

As a seller, we can also work this two-tier market to our advantage. If we can hook a buyer willing to pay both in *cash* and the higher *paper* price, we've gotten ourselves a real bargain.

More likely, however, is that we as a seller can help the buyer with the financing and get the paper price. But, if we're shrewd, we can see to it that another lender actually advances the buyer the money! We do this, for example, by helping the buyer get a Fannie Mae Rollover (Chapter 9) on our property or arranging the best financing possible with a mortgage banker in advance of sale or even obtaining a second mortgage from an institutional lender and having the buyer assume it (see Chapter 6). Here again, we arrange to get all cash for the paper price. There was a time not so many years ago when there was only one price for a house. It didn't make much difference whether the seller took back paper to help the buyer out or if the buyer arranged his or her own financing. Those were the days when interest rates were low, financing was largely amortized for 30 years with true 30-year due dates, and the payments remained fixed for the life of the loan.

Those were simpler days, times when anyone and just about everyone invested in real estate, whether it be a home, a condominium, an apartment building, or whatever. In fact, as we noted earlier, it was the very nature of the easy financing that allowed the prices of real estate to rise to the high levels of this decade.

THE WINNER IN THE NEW MORTGAGE GAME

But, those days are now gone. We can't indulge in the memories of the past, but have to deal with the realities of the present. In today's market, with new and sometimes difficult financing, we're not likely to see the rapid jumps in overall prices that we saw in the past. Some houses and other pieces of property are likely to sit endlessly on the market with no buyers.

Do you know which those will be?

I can tell you. They will be the houses, the apartment buildings, the condominiums which do not have the good financing. They will be the properties whose owners really don't understand the "new mortgage game." They will be the properties which are being sold today according to the financing of yesterday.

Hopefully, as a buyer or seller, after reading *The New Mortgage Game,* you will not be involved with those houses. Rather, as a buyer, you will be finding great opportunities and bargains. And as a seller, you will be getting your price and a quick sale.

Today, as never before, financing is the true name of the game.

KEEPING IN TOUCH

The rules of the new mortgage game are constantly changing. Parts of what was true as this was written may have changed by the time you read it. To play the game to win, you need to know the latest information. For that there are a number of newsletters and magazines available which do a good job of reporting on mortgages. The best I have seen is one called, *Real Estate Hotline*. It is available at 100 S. Los Robles Ave., Suite 100, Pasadena, Calif. 91101. My understanding is that they will send anyone who writes and is interested a free sample copy. Their subscription rate is under $40 per year.

INDEX